THE ECONOMICS OF MONETARY INTEGRATION

THE ECONOMICS OF
MONETARY INTEGRATION

PAUL DE GRAUWE

OXFORD UNIVERSITY PRESS

1992

Oxford University Press, Walton Street, Oxford OX2 6DP

Oxford New York Toronto
Delhi Bombay Calcutta Madras Karachi
Petaling Jaya Singapore Hong Kong Tokyo
Nairobi Dar es Salaam Cape Town
Melbourne Auckland
and associated companies in
Berlin Ibadan

Oxford is a trade mark of Oxford University Press

Published in the United States
by Oxford University Press, New York

British Library Cataloguing in Publication Data
data available

Library of Congress Cataloging in Publication Data
Grauwe, Paul de.
The economics of monetary integration / Paul de Grauwe.
Includes bibliographical references.
1. Monetary unions—European Economic Community countries.
2. Monetary policy—European Economic Community countries.
3. European Monetary System (Organization) I. Title.
HG930.5.G674   1992   332.4'5'094—dc20   91–42193
ISBN 0–19–877347–1
ISBN 0–19–877348–X (pbk.)

Typeset by Hope Services (Abingdon) Ltd
Printed in Great Britain by
Biddles Ltd
Guildford & King's Lynn

Preface

Just a few years ago academic discussions relating to monetary integration had almost completely vanished. The subject seemed dead. The prospects of a monetary union in Europe, which had triggered earlier discussions, looked very dim. The prevailing academic and non-academic view was that monetary union in Europe was too far away to be worth thinking about.

Things changed very quickly in the middle of the 1980s. A new political momentum was created favouring drastic new initiatives towards economic integration in Europe. Thanks to the Delors Report, which was published in 1989, thinking about monetary integration was made respectable again. Academic studies about the subject became a boom industry.

This book attempts to bring together both the old literature on monetary integration, which was developed in the 1960s and the early 1970s, and the new literature which started to flourish from the middle of the 1980s. As the reader will discover, the confrontation of these two strands of the literature on monetary integration has allowed us to obtain new and exciting insights, which are also important to the policy-maker.

The first part of the book is entirely devoted to what is now called the theory of optimum currency areas. This theory analyses the costs and benefits for nations of joining a monetary union. The basic insights of this theory were developed in the 1960s. Generally speaking this theory led to some scepticism about the benefits of monetary union. The recent literature, however, emphasizing issues of credibility, is much less pessimistic. An attempt is made at integrating these two views.

In the second part of the book we discuss issues relating to the process that leads to monetary integration. Problems that are studied in this part are the transition to monetary union, the workings of 'incomplete' monetary unions (like the European Monetary System), the setting-up of a common central bank, and fiscal policies in a monetary union.

This book owes a lot to the criticism and comments of many

Preface

colleagues who read previous versions of the manuscript. In particular, I am grateful to Filip Abraham, Michael Artis, Bernard Delbecque, Michele Fratianni, Wolfgang Gebauer, Daniel Gros, Ivo Maes, Wim Moesen and Jürgen von Hagen. My gratitude also goes to Gudrun Heyde who patiently checked the manuscript and suggested many improvements in the text. Finally, I am grateful to Francine Duysens for her excellent secretarial help.

Leuven   P.D.G.
June 1991

Contents

viii   Contents

Contents

ix

List of Figures

List of Tables

Introduction

Is there a good *economic* case for countries to have separate currencies? Does a nation increase its welfare when it abolishes its national currency and adopts some currency of a wider area?

Many European citizens today tend to give positive answers to these questions. The mood in Europe towards monetary union is positive. The answer to these questions, however, is not obvious. There are benefits *and* costs to a monetary union.

The question of whether a nation gains by relinquishing its national currency leads immediately to a new question. Suppose Europeans conclude that it would be good economics to eliminate national currencies: Where do they stop then? Should they have one money for the Benelux, or for the EC, or for the whole of Europe, or maybe for the whole world? This problem leads us to raise the question of what constitutes an optimal monetary area.

In order to tackle all these problems we have to analyse systematically what the costs and benefits are of having one currency. In the first part of this book we will analyse these issues. We will study the *economic* costs and benefits exclusively. There is also much to be said about the political costs and benefits. These, however, are outside the scope of this book.

In the first part of the book the focus is on *complete* monetary unions, i.e. a system in which countries abolish their national currencies and substitute a common currency. In the second part we study how *incomplete* monetary unions function. We analyse how monetary systems operate in which national monetary authorities maintain their national currencies but agree to fix their exchange rates (rigidly or less rigidly). This will lead us to an analysis of the European Monetary System. In this second part we also focus on issues relating to the transition to a full monetary union. How should the transition process to a full monetary union be managed? Should this transition be gradual or sudden? What is the nature of the institutions (including the European central bank) that will have to be created? These questions are still hotly debated, and of great importance. The answer to these questions will also determine how successful the future monetary union will be.

PART I

Costs and Benefits of Monetary Union

1

The Costs of a Common Currency

The costs of a monetary union derive from the fact that when a country relinquishes its national currency, it also relinquishes an instrument of economic policy, i.e. it loses the ability to conduct a national monetary policy. In other words, in a full monetary union the national central bank either ceases to exist or will have no real power. This implies that a nation joining a monetary union will not be able any more to change the price of its currency (by devaluations and revaluations), or to determine the quantity of the national money in circulation.

One may raise the issue here of what good it does for a nation to be able to conduct an independent monetary policy (including changing the price of its currency). There are many situations in which these policies can be very useful for an individual nation. The use of the exchange rate as a policy instrument, for example, is useful because nations are different in some important senses, requiring changes in the exchange rate to occur. In the next section we first analyse some of these differences that may require exchange rate adjustments. In later sections we analyse how the loss of monetary independence may be costly in some other ways for an individual nation.

The analysis that follows in this chapter is known as the 'theory of optimum currency areas'. This theory which has been pioneered by Mundell (1961), McKinnon (1963), and Kenen (1969) has concentrated on the cost side of the cost–benefit analysis of a monetary union.[1]

---

[1] For surveys of this literature, see Ishiyama (1975) and Tower and Willett (1976).

1. Shifts in Demand (Mundell)

Consider the case of a demand shift developed by Mundell in his celebrated article on optimum currency areas.[2] Let us suppose that for some reason EC consumers shift their preferences away from French-made to German-made products. We present the effects of this shift in aggregate demand in Fig. 1.1.

The curves in Fig. 1.1 are the standard aggregate demand and supply curves in an open economy of most macroeconomics textbooks.[3] The demand curve is the negatively sloped line indicating that when the domestic price level increases the demand for the domestic output declines.[4]

The supply curve expresses the idea that when the price of the domestic output increases, domestic firms will increase their supply, to profit from the higher price. These supply curves therefore assume competition in the output markets. In addition, each supply curve is drawn under the assumption that the nominal wage rate and the price of other inputs (e.g. energy, imported inputs) remains constant. Changes in the prices of these inputs will shift these supply curves.

The demand shift is represented by an upward movement of the demand curve in Germany, and a downward movement in France. The result is that output declines in France and that it increases in Germany. This is most likely to lead to additional unemployment in France and a decline of unemployment in Germany.

The effects on the current accounts of the two countries can also be analysed using Fig. 1.1. We first note that the current account is defined as follows:

current account = domestic output − domestic spending

where these variables are expressed in money terms.

---

[2] See Mundell (1961).

[3] See Dornbusch and Fischer (1978) or Parkin and Bade (1988).

[4] This is the substitution effect of a price increase. In the standard aggregate demand analysis, there is also a monetary effect: when the domestic price level increases, the stock of real cash balances declines, leading to an upward movement in the domestic real interest rate. This in turn reduces aggregate demand (see P. De Grauwe, 1983). Here we disregard the monetary effect and concentrate on the substitution effect.

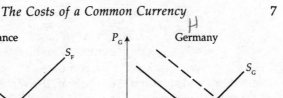

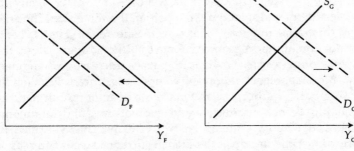

FIG. 1.1 Aggregate demand and supply in France and Germany

In France the value of domestic output has declined as a result of the shift in aggregate demand. If spending by French residents does not decline by the same amount, France will have a current account deficit. This is the most likely outcome, since the social security system automatically pays unemployment benefits. As a result, the disposable income of French residents does not decline to the same extent as output falls. The counterpart of all this is an increase in the French government budget deficit.

In Germany the situation will be the reverse. The value of output increases. It is most likely that the value of total spending by German residents will not increase to the same extent. Part of the extra disposable income is likely to be saved. As a result, Germany will show a surplus on its current account.

Both countries will have an adjustment problem. France is plagued with unemployment and a current account deficit. Germany experiences a boom which also leads to upward pressures on its price level, and it accumulates current account surpluses. The question that arises is whether there is a mechanism that leads to automatic equilibration, without the countries having to resort to devaluations and revaluations?

The answer is positive. There are two mechanisms that will automatically bring back equilibrium in the two countries. One is based on wage flexibility, the other on the mobility of labour.

(1) Wage flexibility. If wages in France and Germany are flexible the following will happen. French workers who are unemployed will reduce their wage claims. In Germany the excess demand for labour will push up the wage rate. The effect of this adjustment mechanism is shown in Fig. 1.2. The reduction of the wage rate in France shifts the aggregate supply curve downwards, whereas the wage increases in Germany shift the aggregate supply curve upwards. These shifts tend to bring back equilibrium. In France the price of output declines, making French products more competitive, and stimulating demand. The opposite occurs in Germany. This adjustment at the same time improves the French current account and reduces the German current account surplus.

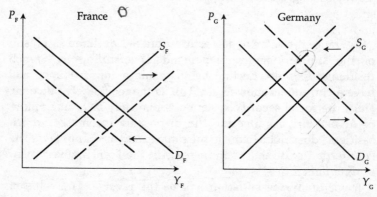

FIG. 1.2 Automatic adjustment process

Note also that the second-order effects on aggregate demand will reinforce the equilibrating mechanism. The wage and price increases in Germany make French products more competitive. This leads to an upward shift in the French aggregate demand curve. Similarly, the decline in French costs and prices makes German products less competitive and shifts the German aggregate demand curve downwards.

(2) Mobility of labour. A second mechanism that will lead to a new equilibrium involves mobility of labour. The French unemployed workers move to Germany where there is excess demand for labour. This movement of labour eliminates the

need to let wages decline in France and increase in Germany. Thus, the French unemployment problem disappears, whereas the inflationary wage pressures in Germany vanish. At the same time the current account disequilibria will also decline. The reason is that the French unemployed were spending on goods and services before without producing anything. This problem tends to disappear with the emigration of the French workers to Germany.

Thus, in principle the adjustment problem for France and Germany will disappear automatically if wages are flexible, and/or if the mobility of labour between the two countries is sufficiently high. If these conditions are not satisfied, however, the adjustment problem will not vanish. Suppose, for example, that wages in France do not decline despite the unemployment situation, and that French workers do not move to Germany. In that case France is stuck in the disequilibrium situation as depicted in Fig. 1.1. In Germany, the excess demand for labour puts upward pressure on the wage rate, producing an upward shift on the supply curve. The adjustment to the disequilibrium must now come exclusively through price increases in Germany. These German price increases make French goods more competitive again, leading to an upward shift in the aggregate demand curve in France. Thus, if wages do not decline in France the adjustment to the disequilibrium will take the form of inflation in Germany.

The German authorities will now face a *dilemma* situation. If they care about inflation, they will want to resist these inflationary pressures (e.g. by restrictive monetary and fiscal policies). However, in that case the current account surplus (which is also the current account deficit of France) will not disappear. If they want to eliminate the current account surplus, the German authorities will have to accept the higher inflation.

This dilemma can only be solved by revaluing the mark against the franc. The effects of this exchange rate adjustment are shown in Fig. 1.3. The revaluation of the mark reduces aggregate demand in Germany, so that the demand curve shifts back to the left. In France the opposite occurs. The devaluation of the franc increases the competitiveness of the French products. This shifts the French aggregate demand curve upwards.

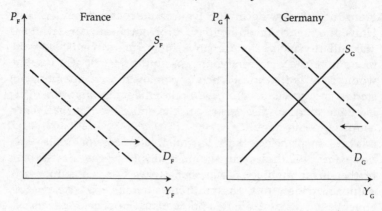

FIG. 1.3 Effects of a revaluation of the DM

The effects of these demand shifts is that France solves its unemployment problem, and that Germany avoids having to accept inflationary pressures. At the same time, the current account deficit of France and surplus of Germany tend to disappear. This remarkable feat is achieved using just one instrument. (The reader may sense that this is too good to be true. And indeed it is. However, for the moment we just present Mundell's theory. We come back later with criticism.)

If France has relinquished the control over its exchange rate by joining a monetary union with Germany, it will be saddled with a sustained unemployment problem, and a current account deficit that can only disappear by deflation in France. In this sense we can say that a monetary union has a cost for France when it is faced with a negative demand shock. Similarly, Germany will find it costly to be in a monetary union with France, because it will have to accept more inflation than it would like.

Can we solve the dilemma in which the two countries find themselves by using other instruments? The answer, in principle, is yes. The German authorities could increase taxes in Germany so as to reduce aggregate demand. (The aggregate demand curve shifts downwards as it does when the mark is revalued.) These tax revenues are then transferred to France where they are spent. (The aggregate demand curve shifts upwards in

France.) France would still have a current account deficit. However, it is financed by the transfer from Germany.

It will be obvious that this solution to the problem is difficult to contemplate between sovereign nations, especially since it would have to be repeated every year if the demand shift that started the problem is a permanent one. This solution, however, is frequently applied between regions of the same nation. Many countries have implicit or explicit regional redistribution schemes through the federal budget. *Implicit* regional redistribution within a nation occurs because of the fact that a large part of the government budget is centralized. As a result, when output declines in a region, the tax revenue of the federal government from this region declines. At the same time, however, the social security system (which is quite often also centralized) will increase transfers to this region (e.g. unemployment benefits). The net result of all this is that the central budget automatically redistributes in favour of regions whose income declines. In some federal states there also exist *explicit* regional redistribution schemes. Probably the best known of these is the German system of 'Finanzausgleich'. This system is described in Box 1.

Let us *recapitulate* the main points developed in this section. If wages are rigid and if labour mobility is limited, countries that form a monetary union will find it harder to adjust to demand shifts than countries that have maintained their own national moneys and that can devalue (revalue) their currency. In the latter case, the exchange rate adds some flexibility to a system which is overly rigid. Put differently, a monetary union between two or more countries is optimal if one of the following conditions is satisfied: (*a*) there is sufficient wage flexibility, (*b*) there is sufficient mobility of labour. It also helps to form a monetary union if the budgetary process is sufficiently centralized so that transfers can be organized smoothly (and not after a lot of political bickering) between the countries of the union.

From this analysis one might be tempted to conclude that the conditions for forming a monetary union between, say, France and Germany are most probably not satisfied. This would, however, be too rash a conclusion. We have not yet introduced the benefits of a monetary union. After all, one can only draw

BOX 1   FISCAL EQUALIZATION BETWEEN LÄNDER IN WEST GERMANY

The system came into existence after the Second World War. Its basic philosophy is that Länder (states) whose tax revenues fall below some predetermined range should receive compensation from Länder whose tax revenues exceed that range. The way this range is computed is rather technical (for more detail see Zimmerman (1989)). Simplifying, it consists in first calculating what the normal tax revenue should be for each state. A state whose tax revenues fall below 92% of this norm receives compensation. To cover these transfers the states whose tax revenues exceed the norm by 2% or more contribute to the system. In Table B1.1 we show the amount of redistribution obtained by this system in 1987.

The effect of this system (together with the automatic redistribution resulting from the centralization of the Federal budget) has been to reduce regional income differentials in West Germany. It has also contributed towards a remarkable absence of large regional disparities in West Germany, which contrasts with the relatively large regional inequalities of income observed in countries like Italy and Spain.

Table B1.1 *Amount of redistribution (marks per capita) through the system of* 'Finanzausgleich' *(1987)*

Contributing Länder	
Baden Württemberg	200
Hessen	215
Hamburg	52
Receiving Länder	
Lower Saxony	155
Schleswig–Holstein	234
Bremen	757
Saarland	320
Rheinland–Palatinate	124
Bavaria	0
North Rhine–Westphalia	8

Source: Zimmerman (1989: 390)

conclusions after comparing costs with benefits. In addition, there is some criticism to be levied against the preceding analysis. We will come back to this criticism in Chapter 2.

2. Different Preferences of Countries about Inflation and Unemployment

Countries differ also because they have different preferences. Some countries are less allergic to inflation than others. This may make the introduction of a common currency costly. The importance of these differences has been analysed by Corden (1972) and Giersch (1973). We present the problem using a simple graphical representation due to De Grauwe (1975).

Consider two countries. For a change, let us call them Italy and Germany. In Fig. 1.4 we represent the Phillips curves of these two countries, in the right-hand panels. The vertical axis shows the rate of change of the wage rate, the horizontal axis the unemployment rate. (We assume for a moment that these Phillips curves are stable, i.e. they do not shift as a result of changes in expectations of inflation. The modern reader will have difficulties swallowing this. Let him/her be patient. We will ask the question of how the analysis is affected once we take into account the fact that these Phillips curves are not stable.)

In the left-hand side panels we represent the relation between wage changes and price changes. This relationship can be written as follows for Italy and Germany respectively:

$$\dot{p}_I = \dot{w}_I - \dot{q}_I \tag{1}$$
$$\dot{p}_G = \dot{w}_G - \dot{q}_G \tag{2}$$

where $\dot{p}_I$ and $\dot{p}_G$ are the rates of inflation, $\dot{w}_I$ and $\dot{w}_G$ are the rates of wage increases, and $\dot{q}_I$ and $\dot{q}_G$ are the rates of growth of labour productivity in Italy and Germany. Equations (1) and (2) can be interpreted by an example. Suppose wages increase by 10% and the rate of growth of the productivity of labour increases by 5% in Italy. Then the rate of price increase that maintains the share of profits in total value added unchanged is 5%. Thus equations (1) and (2) can be considered to define the

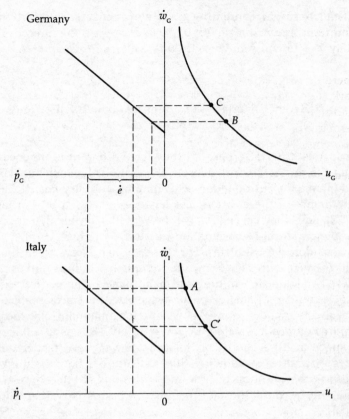

FIG. 1.4 Inflation–unemployment choices in Italy and Germany

rate of price changes that keep profits unchanged (as a percentage of value added).[5] These two equations are represented by the straight lines in the left-hand side panels. Note that the intercept is given by $\dot{q}_I$ and $\dot{q}_G$ respectively. Thus, when the rate of productivity increases in Italy, the line shifts upwards.

[5] Suppose a perfect competitive environment. Then profit maximization implies that $w/p = \partial X/\partial L$. If the production function is Cobb–Douglas, $w/p = \alpha X/L$, where α is the labour share in value added. Taking rates of change yields $w - p = \dot{q}$ (assuming a constant α).

The two countries are linked by the purchasing power parity condition, i.e.

$$\dot{e} = \dot{p}_I - \dot{p}_G \tag{3}$$

where $\dot{e}$ is the rate of depreciation of the lira relative to the mark. Equation (3) should be interpreted as an equilibrium condition. It says that if Italy has a higher rate of inflation than Germany, it will have to depreciate its currency to maintain the competitiveness of its products unchanged. If Italy and Germany decide to form a monetary union, the exchange rate is fixed ($\dot{e} = 0$), so that the rates of inflation must be equal. If this is not the case, e.g. inflation in Italy is higher than in Germany, Italy will increasingly lose competitiveness.

Suppose now that Italy and Germany have different preferences about inflation and unemployment. Italy chooses point A on its Phillips curve, whereas Germany chooses B. It is now immediately obvious that the inflation rates will be different in the two countries, and that a fixed exchange rate will be unsustainable. The cost of a monetary union for the two countries now consists in the fact that if Italy and Germany want to keep the exchange rate fixed they will have to choose another (less preferred) point on their Phillips curves, so that an equal rate of inflation becomes possible. Such an outcome is given by the points C and C' on the respective Phillips curves. (Note that many other points are possible, leading to other joint inflation rates.) Italy now has to accept less inflation and more unemployment than it would do otherwise, Germany has to accept more inflation and less unemployment.

This analysis, which was popular in the 1960s and the early 1970s, has fallen victim to the demise of the Phillips curve. Following the criticisms of Friedman (1968) and Phelps (1968), it is now generally accepted that the Phillips curve is not stable, i.e. that it will shift upwards when expectations of inflation increase. Thus, a country that chooses too high an inflation rate will find that its Phillips curve shifts upwards. Under these conditions the authorities have very little free choice between inflation and unemployment. This has also led to the view that the Phillips curve is really a vertical line in the long run, with far-reaching consequences for the costs of a monetary union.

We show this in Fig. 1.5 where we now represent the long-run vertical Phillips curves. The intercepts with the horizontal line represent the 'natural' rate of unemployment. We observe that the authorities cannot choose an optimal combination of inflation and unemployment. The latter is determined by the natural rate of unemployment and is independent of the inflation rate. There is therefore also nothing to be gained by Italy and Germany from having two different inflation rates. They can set their inflation rates equal to each other by fixing their exchange rates, without any cost in terms of unemployment. Italy and Germany can form a monetary union without costs. Put differently, the fact that Italy and Germany cannot follow independent monetary policies in a monetary union is no loss at all, since an independent monetary policy (and therefore inflation rate) does not bring about lower unemployment.

This analysis is now generally accepted. There remains the problem, however, of the short-term costs of joining a monetary union. Although in the long run, countries cannot really choose between inflation and unemployment, the short-run Phillips curve is still alive. That is, countries that want to reduce inflation will most probably be faced with a temporary increase in the unemployment rate. The experiences of the 1980s makes this clear. In Box 2 we present a few case-studies that illustrate how policies of disinflation during the early 1980s led to significant increases in unemployment in major industrial countries.

The problem that arises then is whether the decision to join a monetary union by a country with a high rate of inflation (Italy in our example of Fig. 1.4) may not lead to a temporary but significant unemployment cost. In Fig. 1.4, the decision by Italy to form a monetary union with Germany raises unemployment in Italy from A to C'. Over time the Italian Phillips curve will shift downwards because of lower expectations of inflation. However, during the transition, Italy is faced with high unemployment.

It should be stressed that this cost of disinflating the economy should not necessarily be called a cost of monetary union. If Italy has too high an inflation, it will have to take action to reduce it. It will then face the short-term unemployment cost whether it is part of a monetary union or not. The issue then really boils down to the question of whether it will be less costly for Italy to reduce the rate of inflation when it forms a monetary union with Germany than when it does it alone. This question has been discussed in great detail recently. We shall return to it in Chapter 2 where we discuss issues of credibility of monetary policies.

The model of Fig. 1.5 allows us to highlight another important source of possible differences between countries. Suppose the

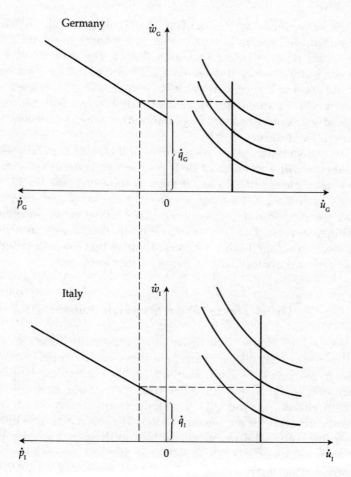

FIG. 1.5 Monetary union in a world of vertical Phillips curves

growth rate of productivity $\dot{q}$ is higher in Germany than in Italy. If both countries decide to form a monetary union this implies that the nominal wage increases in Italy must be lower than in Germany. This can be seen by setting $\dot{e} = 0$ in equation (3), so that $\dot{p}_G = \dot{p}_I$. From equations (1) and (2) it then follows that

$$\dot{w}_G - \dot{q}_G = \dot{w}_I - \dot{q}_I$$

or

$$\dot{w}_G - \dot{w}_I = \dot{q}_G - \dot{q}_I$$

If following monetary unification, the German and the Italian labour unions should centralize their wage bargaining and aim for equal nominal wage increases despite the differences in productivity growth, this would spell trouble. Italian industry would become increasingly less competitive. Therefore, a condition for a successful monetary union is that labour unions should *not* centralize their wage bargaining when productivity growth rates differ.

We can summarize the main points of this section as follows. Countries differ in terms of their preferences towards inflation and unemployment. These differences, however, cannot be a serious obstacle to forming a monetary union, if one accepts that countries cannot really choose an optimal point on their Phillips curves. The only serious issue that arises in this connection is that (high-inflation) countries that join in a union may face a transitory cost in terms of unemployment.

3. Differences in Labour Market Institutions

There is no doubt that there are important institutional differences in the labour markets of European countries. Some labour markets are dominated by highly centralized labour unions (e.g. Germany). In other countries labour unions are decentralized (e.g. the UK). These differences may introduce significant costs for a monetary union. The main reason is that these institutional differences can lead to divergent wage and price developments, even if countries face the same disturbances. For example, when two countries are subjected to the same oil price increase the effect this has on the domestic wages

BOX 2   THE COST OF DISINFLATION: SOME EVIDENCE FROM THE 1980s

Fig. B2.1(d)–(f) presents data on inflation and unemployment in the major industrialized countries during the 1980s. We observe that in all countries the supply shocks of the 1979–80 period led to an increase in the inflation rate. Most countries then started a process of disinflation, which contributed to an increase in the unemployment rate. Some countries (France, Germany, and Italy) experienced significantly more difficulties in reducing their inflation rates, that is, the cost in terms of unemployment seems to have been considerable. In other words it took many years for the respective Phillips curves to move inwards. For France and Italy there was little evidence that these Phillips curves had turned inwards at the end of the 1980s. This suggests two possible interpretations. One is that inflationary expectations were very slow to come down; the other is that the natural rate of unemployment may have increased in these countries.

Countries like the USA and the UK experienced less difficulty in shifting their Phillips curves downwards. In De Grauwe (1990) an interpretation is given of this phenomenon. We return to this issue when we discuss the functioning of the European Monetary System in Chapter 5.

Finally, note the special position of *Japan* which seems to have been able to reduce inflation without any apparent cost in terms of unemployment.

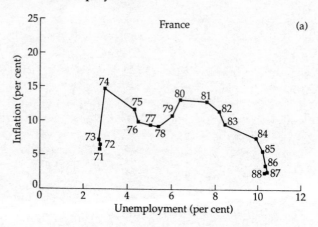

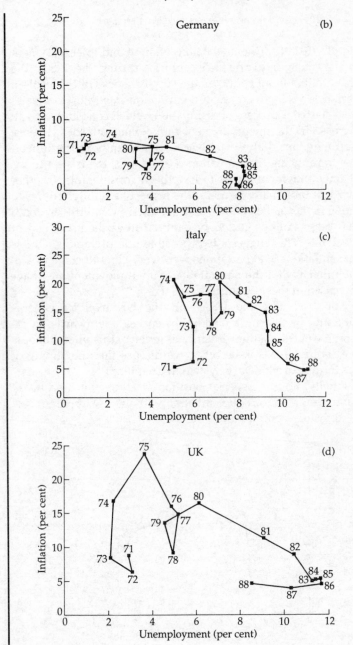

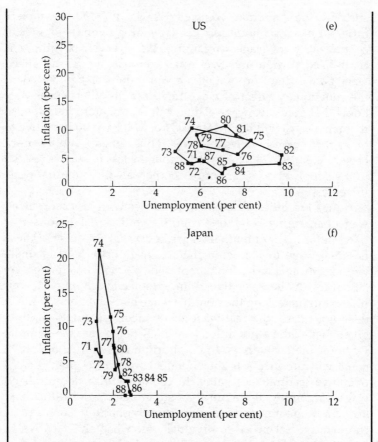

FIG. B2.1 Inflation and unemployment in major industrial countries, 1980s

and prices very much depends on how labour unions react to these shocks.

Recent macroeconomic theories have been developed that shed some light on the importance of labour market institutions. The most popular one was developed by Bruno and Sachs (1985).[6] The idea can be formulated as follows. Supply shocks,

[6] It should be stressed that these theories were already available and widely discussed in many European countries before Bruno and Sachs discovered

such as the one that occurred during 1979–80, have very different macroeconomic effects depending upon the degree of centralization of wage bargaining. When wage bargaining is centralized (Bruno and Sachs call countries with centralized wage bargaining 'corporatist'), labour unions take into account the inflationary effect of wage increases. In other words they know that excessive wage claims will lead to more inflation, so that real wages will not increase. They will have no incentive to make these excessive wage claims. Thus, when a supply shock occurs, as in 1979–80, they realize that the loss in real wages due to the supply shocks cannot be compensated by nominal wage increases.

Things are quite different in countries with less centralized wage bargaining. In these countries individual unions that bargain for higher nominal wages know that the effect of these nominal wage increases on the aggregate price level is small, because these unions only represent a small fraction of the labour force. There is a free-riding problem. Each union has an interest in increasing the nominal wage of its members. For if it does not do so, the real wage of its members would decline, given that all the other unions are likely to increase the nominal wage for their members. In equilibrium this non-co-operative game will produce a higher nominal wage level than the co-operative (centralized) game. In countries with decentralized wage bargaining therefore it is structurally more difficult to arrive at wage moderation after a supply shock. In such a non-co-operative set-up no individual union has an incentive to take the first step in reducing its nominal wage claim. For it risks that the others will not follow, so that the real wage level of its members will decline.

The analogy with the spectators in a football stadium is well known. When they are all seated, the individual spectator has an incentive to stand up so as to have a better view of the game. The dynamics of this game is that they all stand up, see no better, and are more uncomfortable. Once they stand up, it is equally difficult to induce them to sit down. The individual who takes the first step and sits down will see nothing, as long

them. Their advantage was that they wrote in English, and thereby succeeded in disseminating the idea internationally.

as the others do not follow his example. Since he is sitting, most spectators in the stadium will not even notice this good example.

This co-operation story has recently been extended by Calmfors and Driffill (1988) who noted that the relationship between centralization of wage bargaining and outcomes is not a linear process. In particular, the more we move towards the decentralized spectrum the more another externality comes to play a role. For in a very decentralized system (e.g. wage bargaining at the firm level), the wage claims will have a direct effect on the competitiveness of the firm, and therefore on the employment prospects of individual union members. Excessive wage claims by an individual union will lead to a strong reduction of employment. Thus, when faced with a supply shock, unions in such a decentralized system may exhibit a considerable degree of wage restraint.

This insight then leads to the conclusion that countries with either strong centralization or strong decentralization of wage bargaining are better equipped to face supply shocks such as the one that occurred during 1979–80 than countries with an intermediate degree of centralization. In these 'extreme' countries there will be a greater wage moderation than in the intermediate countries. As a result, the countries with extreme centralization or decentralization tend to fare better, in terms of inflation and unemployment, following supply shocks, than the others.

Some empirical evidence for this hypothesis is shown in Fig. 1.6. On the horizontal axis we show the degree of centralization of labour markets in a group of industrial countries. (These indices were computed by Calmfors and Driffill (1988).) On the vertical axis the changes in the 'misery' indices of the same countries from the 1970s to the 1980s are represented. These misery indices are the sum of the inflation rate and the unemployment rate.[7] One can see that intermediate countries seem to have experienced a greater worsening of their misery indices than the countries with extreme centralization or decentralization. In other words the labour market institutions

---

[7] In De Grauwe (1990) econometric evidence is presented giving some support to the non-linear relationship between economic performance and the degree of centralization of labour markets.

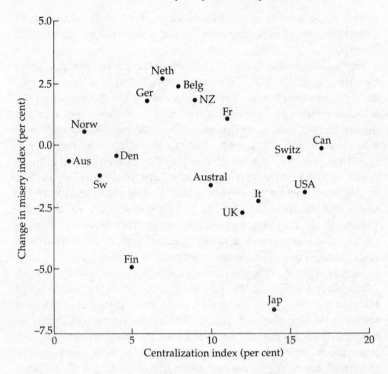

FIG. 1.6 Change in misery indices (from the 1970s to the 1980s) and labour market centralization

Note: The misery index is the sum of the inflation rate and the unemployment rate. The change in the index is measured from 1973–9 to 1980–8. The centralization index measures the degree of centralization of labour unions. A *low* number implies a *high* degree of centralization.

Source: Misery index computed from OECD, *Economic Outlook*; index of centralization of wage bargaining from Calmfors and Driffill (1988).

of these countries may have made it more difficult to reduce inflation without losses in output following the supply shocks of 1979–80.

It follows that a country might find itself in a situation where wages and prices increase faster than in other countries even when the shock that triggered it all is the same. In terms of the two-country model that we used in section 1 the supply curve in one country shifts upwards more than in the other country. This will lead to macroeconomic adjustment problems that are of the same nature as the ones we analysed in section 1.

We conclude that countries with very different labour market institutions may find it costly to form a monetary union. With each supply shock, wages and prices in these countries may be affected differently, making it difficult to correct for these differences when the exchange rate is irrevocably fixed.

4. Growth Rates are Different

Some countries grow faster than others. This is made clear in Table 1.1. We find that during the 1980s the southern European countries (and Ireland) experienced growth rates of their GDP which were significantly higher than in the northern part of Europe. (The same phenomenon is observed during the 1970s.)

Such differences in growth rates could lead to a problem when countries form a monetary union. We illustrate it with the following example. Country A's GDP is growing at 5% per year, country B's GDP at 3% per year. Suppose that the income elasticity of A's imports from B is one, and that similarly B's income elasticity of imports from A is equal to one. Then country A's imports from B will grow at 5% per year, whereas B's imports from A will grow at only 3% per year. This will lead

TABLE 1.1 *Average yearly growth rates of GDP in the EC, 1981–1990*

Belgium	1.9
France	2.1
Germany	2.1
Ireland	2.8
Italy	2.5
Netherlands	1.8
Portugal	2.7
Spain	2.9

Source: EC Commission (1990).

to a trade balance problem of the fast-growing country A, whose imports tend to grow faster than its exports.

In order to avoid chronic deficits of its trade account, country A will have to reduce the price of its exports to country B, so that the latter country increases its purchases of goods from country A. In other words, country A's terms of trade must decline so as to make its products more competitive. Country A can do this in two ways: a depreciation of the currency or a lower rate of domestic price increases than in country B. If it joins a monetary union with country B, however, only the second option will be available. This will require country A to follow relatively deflationary policies, which in turn will constrain the growth process. Thus, a monetary union has a cost for the fast-growing country. It will find it more advantageous to keep its national currency, so as to have the option of depreciating its currency when it finds itself constrained by unfavourable developments in its trade account.

5. Different Fiscal Systems and the Seigniorage Problem

Countries differ also because they have different fiscal systems. These differences often lead countries to use different combinations of debt and monetary financing of the government budget deficit. When these countries join a monetary union, they will be constrained in the way they finance their budget deficits.

In order to show this, it is useful to start from the government budget constraint:

$$G - T + rB = dB/dt + dM/dt \qquad (4)$$

where G is the level of government spending (excluding interest payments on the government debt), T is the tax revenue, r is the interest rate on the government debt, B, and M is the level of high-powered money (monetary base).

The left-hand side of equation (4) is the government budget deficit. It consists of the primary budget deficit $(G-T)$ and the interest payment on the government debt (rB). The right-hand side is the financing side. The budget deficit can be financed by issuing debt (dB/dt) or by issuing high-powered money dM/dt.

(In the following we represent the changes per unit of time by putting a dot above a variable, thus $dB/dt=\dot{B}$ and $dM/dt=\dot{M}$).

It is convenient to express variables as ratios to GNP. Let us therefore define

$$b = B/Y \tag{5}$$

where Y is GNP, so that b is the debt to GNP ratio.

This allows us to write

$$\dot{b} = \dot{B}/Y \times B\dot{Y}/Y^2$$

or using (5) and manipulating

$$\dot{B} = \dot{b}Y + b\dot{Y} \tag{6}$$

Substituting (6) into (4) yields

$$\dot{b} = (g - t) + (r - x)b - \dot{m} \tag{7}$$

where $g=G/Y$, $t=T/Y$, $x=\dot{Y}/Y$ (the growth rate of GNP), and $\dot{m}=\dot{M}/Y$.

Equation (7) can be interpreted as follows. When the interest rate on government debt exceeds the growth rate of GNP, the debt to GNP ratio will increase without limitation. The dynamics of debt accumulation can be stopped only if the primary budget deficit (as a per cent of GDP) turns into a surplus ($(g - t)$ then becomes negative). Alternatively, the debt accumulation can be stopped by a sufficiently large revenue from money creation. The latter is also called seigniorage. It is clear, however, that the systematic use of this source of finance will lead to inflation.

The nature of the government budget constraint can also be made clear as follows: One can ask the question under what conditions the debt to GDP ratio will stabilize at a constant value. Equation (7) gives the answer. Set $\dot{b}=0$. This yields

$$(r - x)b = (t - g) + \dot{m} \tag{8}$$

Thus, if the interest rate exceeds the growth rate of the economy, it is necessary that either the primary budget shows a sufficiently high surplus or that money creation is sufficiently high in order to stabilize the debt to GNP ratio.

The theory of optimal public finance now tells us that rational governments will use the different sources of revenue so that the marginal cost of raising revenue through these different means is equalized.[8] Thus, if the marginal cost of raising revenue by increasing taxes exceeds the marginal cost of raising revenue by inflation (seigniorage), it will be optimal to reduce taxes and to increase inflation.

The preceding also means that countries will have different optimal inflation rates. In general, countries with an under-developed tax system will find it more advantageous to raise revenue by inflation (seigniorage). Put differently, a country with an underdeveloped fiscal system experiences large costs in raising revenue by increasing tax rates. It will be less costly to increase government revenue by inflation.

This reasoning leads to the following implication for the costs of a monetary union. Less developed countries that join a monetary union with more developed countries that have a low rate of inflation will also have to lower inflation. This then means that, for a given budget deficit, they will have to increase taxes. There will be a loss of welfare. Some economists (e.g. Dornbusch (1987)) have claimed that this is a particularly acute problem for the southern EC countries. By joining the low-inflation northern monetary zone they will have to increase taxes, or let the deficit increase further. For these countries the cost of the monetary union is that they will have to rely too much on a costly way of raising revenues.

Table 1.2 gives some empirical evidence on the size of the seigniorage for these southern countries, and compares it with Germany. We observe that up to the middle of the 1980s, the southern European countries had high seigniorage revenues. These revenues amounted to 2–3% of GNP in all these countries. This was certainly much more important than in the northern countries. Since the middle of the 1980s, however, seigniorage revenue of these countries has declined significantly, mainly because of the reduction in their inflation rates. This leads to the conclusion that if these countries should join a monetary union with the low-inflation countries today in 1991, the additional cost (in terms of public finance) would probably not be very important.

---

[8] See Stanley Fischer (1982) and Grilli (1989).

TABLE 1.2 *Seigniorage revenues as per cent of GNP*

	1976–85	1986–90
Greece	3.4	1.5
Italy	2.6	0.7
Portugal	3.4	1.9
Spain	2.9	0.8
West Germany	0.2	0.6

Sources: Dornbusch (1987) and Gros (1990).

6. Conclusion

In this chapter we discussed differences between countries. We observed that countries can use exchange rate changes, or other monetary policies, to correct for these differences. We found that in most cases there is an alternative to using the exchange rate as a policy instrument. For example, when confronted with a loss of domestic competitiveness, countries can use contractionary demand policies aiming at regaining competitiveness. However, these alternatives are often more painful, and therefore less desirable. To the extent that these alternative policies are more painful than changing the exchange rate we concluded that the country under consideration does not gain from relinquishing its money and joining a currency union. (Note, however, that we still have not introduced the benefit side of the analysis. It is still possible that even if there are costs associated with relinquishing one's national money, the benefits outweigh these costs.)

The analysis of this chapter which is based on the theory of optimum currency areas has recently been subjected to much criticism. This has led to new and important insights. In the next chapter we turn our attention to this criticism.

2

The Theory of Optimum Currency Areas: A Critique

Introduction

In the previous chapter we analysed the reasons why countries might find it costly to join a monetary union. Recently, this analysis, which is known as the theory of optimum currency areas, has come under criticism.[1] This criticism has been formulated at different levels. First one may question the view that the differences between countries are important enough to bother about. Secondly, the exchange rate instrument may not be very effective in correcting for the differences between nations. Thirdly, not only may the exchange rate be ineffective, it may do more harm than good in the hands of politicians.

In this chapter we analyse this criticism in greater detail.

1. How Relevant are the Differences between Countries?

There is no doubt that countries *are* different. The question, however, is whether these differences are important enough to represent a stumbling-block for monetary unification.

1.1. Is a demand shock concentrated in one country a likely event?

The classical analysis of Mundell started from the scenario in which a demand shift occurs away from the products of one country in favour of another country. Is such a shock likely to occur frequently between the European countries that are planning to form a monetary union? There is a major argument

---

[1] See EC Commission (1990) and Gros and Thygesen (1991).

that leads us to conclude that such differential shocks in demand may occur less frequently in a future European monetary union.

Trade between the industrial European nations is to a large degree intra-industry trade. This trade is based on the existence of economies of scale and imperfect competition (product differentiation). It leads to a structure of trade in which countries buy and sell to each other the same categories of products. Thus, France sells cars to and buys cars from Germany. And so does Germany. This structure of trade leads to a situation where most demand shocks will affect these countries in a similar way. For example, when consumers reduce their demand for cars, they will buy fewer French *and* German cars. Thus, both countries' aggregate demand will be affected in similar ways.

The removal of barriers with the completion of the single market will reinforce these tendencies. As a result, most demand shocks will tend to have similar effects.[2] Instead of being asymmetric, these shocks will tend to be more symmetric.

Does this mean that we can discard Mundell's analysis of asymmetric demand shocks as irrelevant for the process of European monetary integration? Not necessarily. There is another feature of the dynamics of trade with economies of scale that may make Mundell's analysis very relevant. Trade integration which occurs as a result of economies of scale also leads to regional concentration of industrial activities.[3] The basic argument here is that when impediments to trade decline this has two opposing effects on the localization of industries. It makes it possible to produce closer to the final markets, but it also makes it possible to concentrate production so as to profit from economies of scale (both static and dynamic). This explains why trade integration in fact may lead to more concentration of regional activities rather than less.

The fact that trade may lead to regional concentration of industrial activities is illustrated rather dramatically by comparing

---

[2] Peter Kenen (1969) also stressed the importance of the similarity of the trading structure for making a monetary union less costly.

[3] This is an old idea that was developed by Myrdal (1957) and Kaldor (1966). For a survey see Balassa (1961). Krugman gives a more rigorous underpinning of these ideas in some of his recent writing. See Krugman (1991).

the regional distribution of the automobile production in the USA and in Europe (see Table 2.1). The most striking feature of this table is that the US production of automobiles is much more regionally concentrated than the EC's. (This feature is found in many other industrial sectors, see Krugman (1991)). There is also no doubt that the US market is more highly integrated than the EC market, i.e. there are fewer impediments to trade in the USA than in the EC. This evidence therefore suggests that when the EC moves forward in the direction of a truly integrated market, it may experience similar kinds of regional concentrations of economic activities as those observed in the USA today. It is therefore not to be excluded that the automobile industry, for example, will tend to be more concentrated in say Germany (although we are not sure it will be Germany, it could also be another country). Sector-specific shocks may then become country-specific shocks. Countries faced with these shocks may then prefer to use the exchange rate as an instrument of economic policy to correct for these disturbances.

TABLE 2.1 *Distribution of auto production*

	USA		EC
Midwest	66.3	Germany	38.5
South	25.4	France	31.1
West	5.1	Italy	17.6
North-east	3.2	UK	12.9

Source: Paul Krugman (1991).

We conclude here that further trade integration in Europe has an ambiguous effect on the likelihood that demand shocks will tend to be asymmetric between countries. We should not discard the possibility that in a more integrated Europe, negative demand shocks will be concentrated on one country, because that country has a large concentration of the activities of one industry.

1.2. *Institutional differences in labour markets*

The differences in the workings of the labour markets in different countries are well documented. These differences, however, have accumulated over the years, partly because European countries have experienced separate policy regimes. The issue is whether monetary integration will not drastically change the behaviour of labour unions, so that the differences we observe today may disappear.[4]

An example may clarify this point. In Fig. 2.1 we present the labour markets of two countries that are candidates for a monetary union. The figure is based on the model of McDonald and Solow (1981).[5] On the vertical axis we have the real wage level, on the horizontal axis the level of employment (N). The convex curves are the indifference curves of the labour union. It is assumed that there is only one labour union in each country. The union maximizes its utility which depends on both the real wage level and the employment of its members. The negatively sloped line is the economy-wide demand-for-labour curve. For the union, which maximizes its utility, the demand-for-labour curve is a constraint: thus, the union will select a point on it which maximizes its utility. This is represented in Fig. 2.1 by the points A and B.

The interesting feature of this model is that the employment line takes into account the reaction of the authorities to what the labour unions are doing. If we assume that the authorities give a higher weight to employment in their utility function than the labour unions, we may have the following situation. When the labour unions set a wage that reduces the employment level below the level that the authorities find optimal, they will react by changing their policies. For example, they will engage in more expansionary monetary and fiscal policies to absorb the unemployed, they may create public jobs, etc. To the extent that labour unions take this reaction of the authorities into account, the constraint the unions face will change. More specifically, the employment line becomes steeper because an increase in the real wage level reduces private employment and, thus, induces the authorities to intensify their job-creating policies. As a

---

[4] See Gros and Thygesen (1991), ch. 9.
[5] For a discussion of this model see Carlin and Soskice (1990).

result, an increase in the real wage level has a less pronounced effect on the total level of employment.[6] Thus, the steepness of this employment line also reflects the willingness of the authorities to engage in expansionary employment policies when the wage rate increases.

In Fig. 2.1 we have drawn the employment line of country B steeper than that of country A, assuming that the authorities of country B are more willing to accommodate the union's wage-setting behaviour by expansionary employment policies. Monetary union now will change the possibility for the national governments to follow such accommodating policies. Monetary policies will now be centralized, so that the unions of the two countries face the same reactions of the monetary authorities. This will make the employment lines similar, so that the two unions will tend to select a similar combination of wage rates and employment levels.

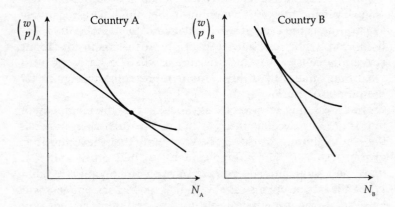

FIG. 2.1 The Solow–MacDonald model in two countries

The differences, however, are unlikely to disappear completely. National governments have other employment policies at their disposal besides monetary policies. For example, they can create jobs in the government sector, financing these extra expenditures by issuing debt. A monetary union does not

---

[6] This employment line must in fact be interpreted as the reaction curve of the government. The union operates as a 'Stackelberg' leader and selects the optimal point on this reaction line.

necessarily constrain this accommodating government behaviour. Thus, although the differences in the behaviour of the labour unions will be less pronounced, they will certainly not be eliminated completely.

Finally, it should also be stressed that the previous analysis assumes a completely centralized union in both countries. As pointed out earlier, unions are different across countries because of different degrees of centralization. It is not clear how monetary union will change these institutional differences.

We conclude that the institutional differences in the national labour markets will continue to exist for quite some time after the introduction of a common currency. This may lead to divergent wage and employment tendencies, and severe adjustment problems when the exchange rate instrument has disappeared.

1.3. *Do differences in growth rates matter?*

Fast-growing countries experience fast-growing imports. In order to allow exports to increase at the same rate, these countries will have to make their exports more competitive by real depreciations of their currencies. If they join a monetary union, this will be made more difficult. As a result, these countries will be constrained in their growth. This popular view of the constraint imposed on fast-growing countries that decide to join a monetary union has very little empirical support.

In Fig. 2.2 we present data (as collected by the EC Commission (1990), 147) on the growth rates of EC countries during 1973–88 and their real depreciations (or appreciations). The high-growers are above the horizontal line, the low-growers below. We observe that among the fast-growers there are countries that saw their currency appreciate and others depreciate. The same is true for the slow-growers.[7]

---

[7] This visual evidence is confirmed by the regression equation that the Commission (1990: 146) computed:

$$GDP = 0.36 + 0.095*REER \qquad \text{Corrected } R^2 = -0.02$$
$$\quad\;\;(0.30)\;\;(0.105)$$

where GDP = growth rate of GDP minus EC growth, and REER = the average growth rate of unit labour costs relative to Community partners. Standard errors

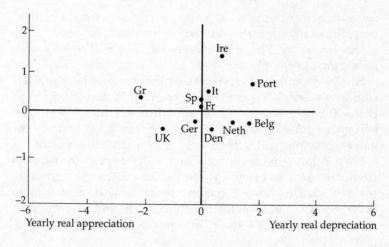

FIG. 2.2 Real depreciation and growth, 1973–1988
Source: EC Commission (1990: 147)

This lack of relation between economic growth and real depreciations has been given an elegant interpretation recently by Paul Krugman (1989). Economic growth has relatively little to do with the static view implicit in the story told in the earlier sections. Economic growth implies mostly the development of new products. Fast-growing countries are those that are able to develop new products, or old products with new qualitative features. The result of this growth process is that the income elasticities of the exports of fast-growing countries are typically higher than those of slow-growers. More importantly, these income elasticities of the export goods of the fast-growers will also typically be higher than the income elasticities of their imports. (See Krugman (1989) for empirical evidence.) As a result, these countries can grow faster without incurring trade balance problems. This also implies that the fast-growers can increase their exports at a fast pace without having to resort to real depreciations.

There is a second reason why the fast-growing countries should not worry too much that joining a monetary union will

are in brackets. It can be seen that the coefficient of REER is not statistically different from zero.

constrain their potential for growth. This has to do with the existence of capital flows. A fast-growing country is usually also a country where the productivity of capital is higher than in slow-growing countries. This difference in the productivity of capital will induce investment flows from the slow-growing countries to the fast-growing countries. These capital flows then make it possible for the fast-growing country to finance current account deficits without any need to devalue the currency.

There is even an argument to be made here that fast-growing countries that join a monetary union with slow-growing countries will find it easier to attract foreign capital. With no exchange rate uncertainty, investors from the slow-growing area may be more forthcoming in moving their capital to the high-growing country in order to profit from the larger returns.

One can conclude that differences in the growth rates of countries cannot really be considered as an obstacle to monetary integration. In other words, fast-growing countries will, in general, not have to reduce their growth rates by joining a monetary union.

2. Nominal and Real Depreciations of the Currency

The cost of relinquishing one's national currency lies in the fact that a country cannot change its exchange rate any more to correct for differential developments in demand, or in costs and prices. The question, however, is whether these exchange rate changes are effective in making such corrections. Put differently, the question that arises is whether *nominal* exchange rate changes can permanently alter the *real* exchange rates of the country.

This is a crucial question. For if the answer is negative, one can conclude that countries, even if they develop important differences between themselves, would not have to meet extra costs when joining a monetary union. The instrument they lose does not really allow them to correct for these differences.

In order to analyse this question of the effectiveness of exchange rate changes we return to two of the asymmetric disturbances analysed in the previous chapter.

2.1. *Devaluations to correct for asymmetric demand shocks*

Let us take the case of France developed in section 1.1 of the previous chapter. We assumed that a shift occurred away from French products in favour of German products. In order to cope with this problem France devalues its currency. We present the situation in Fig. 2.3. As a result of the devaluation aggregate demand in France shifts back upwards and corrects for the initial unfavourable demand shift. The new equilibrium point is F.

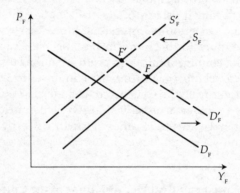

FIG. 2.3 Price and cost effects of a devaluation

It is unlikely that this new equilibrium point can be sustained. The reason is that the devaluation raises the price of imported goods. This raises the cost of production directly. It also will increase the nominal wage level in France as workers are likely to be compensated for the loss of purchasing power. All this means that the aggregate supply curve will shift upwards. Thus, prices increase and output declines. These price increases feed back again into the wage-formation process and lead to further upward movements of the aggregate supply curve. The final equilibrium will be located at a point like F'. The initial favourable effects of the devaluation tend to disappear over time. It is not possible to say here whether these favourable effects of the devaluation on output will disappear completely. This depends on the openness of the economy, on the degree to which wage-earners will adjust their wage claims to correct for the loss of purchasing power. There is a lot of empirical evidence, however, that for most of the European countries this withering away of the initially favourable effects of a devaluation will be strong.[8]

The previous conclusion can also be phrased as follows. Nominal exchange rate changes have only temporary effects on the competitiveness of countries. Over time the nominal devaluation leads to domestic cost and price increases which tend to restore the initial competitiveness. In other words, nominal devaluations only lead to temporary *real* devaluations. In the long run nominal exchange rate changes do not affect the real exchange rate of a country.

Does this conclusion about the long-run ineffectiveness of exchange rate changes imply that countries do not lose anything by relinquishing this instrument? The answer is negative. We also have to analyse the short-term effects of an exchange rate policy aiming at correcting the initial disturbance, and we have to compare these to alternative policies that will have to be followed in the absence of a devaluation. This is done in Fig. 2.4. We have added here a line (*TT*) which expresses the

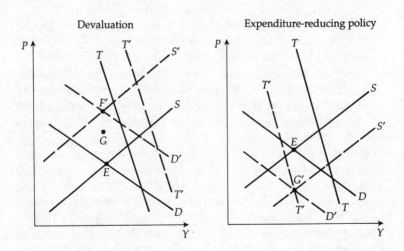

Fig. 2.4 Devaluation and deflationary policies compared

[8] See EC Commission (1990), ch. 6.

trade account equilibrium condition. It is derived as follows. Trade account equilibrium is defined as equality between the value of domestic output and the value of spending by residents (sometimes also called absorption). Thus we have equilibrium in the trade account if and only if:

$$P_d Y = P_a A \tag{9}$$

Where P_d is the price of the domestic good, Y the domestic output level, P_a is the average price index of the domestic and the imported good, A is absorption (in real terms). The level of real absorption depends on many factors (e.g. government spending, the real interest rate). If these are fixed, we can derive a negative relation between P_d and Y which maintains the equality (9), in other words which maintains trade account equilibrium. The negative relationship follows from the fact that as P_d increases, P_a (which contains the import price) increases less than proportionately, so that the left-hand side increases relative to the right-hand side of (9). Thus, when P_d increases, the value of output increases relative to the value of absorption, tending to produce a trade account surplus. It follows that domestic output should decline to maintain trade account equilibrium. Put differently an increase in P_d (for a given import price) is equivalent to an improvement in the terms of trade. This allows the country to reduce domestic output and still maintain equilibrium in the trade account.

Points to the left of this TT-line are ones where the country has a trade deficit, i.e. the level of domestic output is too low compared to the level of absorption. Points to the right of the TT-line are those where the country produces more than it spends.

In Fig. 2.4, we assume that the country has been hit by a negative demand shock which has brought the output point to E. As a result, the country has a trade account deficit which will have to be corrected. One way to correct the disequilibrium is to devalue the currency. The dynamics of the adjustment after the devaluation is shown in the left-hand panel of Fig. 2.4. The devaluation shifts the demand and the supply curves upwards, as explained earlier. However, it also shifts the TT-curve to the right (to TT'). This follows from the fact that the devaluation increases the price of imports. Thus, in equation (9), P_a

increases. It follows that P_d and/or Y must increase to maintain trade account equilibrium (at least if the real level of absorption A remains unchanged).

The new equilibrium in the goods market is now located at point F'. It can be seen that there is still a trade account deficit because the new output point is located to the left of the TT' line. In order to restore trade account equilibrium, the government will have to follow policies reducing real absorption. These policies have the effect of shifting the TT'-line to the left. The reason is that with a lower level of absorption (due to say lower government spending) the level of output that maintains trade account equilibrium is also reduced. These expenditure-reducing policies also affect the demand curve, however. In general expenditure-reducing policies reduce domestic demand for the domestic good. It can be shown that there exists a combination of devaluation and expenditure-reducing policy that will bring the economy to a point like G, located vertically above the initial output point.[9] In the end the devaluation is neutral in that it does not affect output permanently.

In the right-hand panel of Fig. 2.4 we present the case where the country chooses *not* to devalue. Since in the initial situation (point E) there is a trade account deficit, the authorities will have to do something to correct this. This will necessarily have to be a policy which reduces absorption. Thus, deflationary monetary and/or fiscal policies will have to be instituted. These shift the trade account equilibrium line TT to the left.

These expenditure-reducing policies, however, also reduce aggregate demand for the domestic goods. Thus, the aggregate demand line also shifts to the left. The economy will go through a deflationary process, which reduces output. With sufficient wage and price flexibility, this will also tend to shift the supply line downwards, because the decline in prices leads to lower nominal wages. If wages and prices are not very flexible, this may require a considerable time. In the long run, the economy will settle at a point like G'. The output level is equal to its initial level, and the trade account is in equilibrium.

We conclude that in *the long run* the two policies (devaluation and expenditure-reducing) lead to the same effect on output

---

[9] See De Grauwe (1983), ch. 9.

and the trade account. Put differently, in the long run the exchange rate will not solve problems that arise from differences between countries that originate in the goods markets. This result is also in the tradition of the classical economists. These stressed that money is a veil. Structural differences should be tackled with structural policies. Manipulating money (its quantity or its price) cannot change these real differences.

The difference between the two policies, a devaluation or an expenditure-reducing policy, is to be found in their *short-term dynamics*. When the country devalues, it avoids the severe deflationary effects on domestic output during the transition. The cost of this policy is that there will be inflation. With the second policy, inflation is avoided. The cost, however, is that output declines during the transition period. In addition, as we have seen, this second policy may take a long time to be successful if the degree of wage and price flexibility is limited.

One can conclude that although a devaluation does not have a permanent effect on competitiveness and output, its dynamics will be quite different from the dynamics engendered by the alternative policy which will necessarily have to be followed if the country has relinquished control over its national money. This loss of a policy instrument will be a cost of the monetary union.

In Box 3 we present a case-study of a recent devaluation (Belgium in 1982) that helped this country to restore domestic and trade account equilibrium at a cost that was most probably lower than if it had not used the exchange rate instrument. There were other noteworthy and successful devaluations during the 1980s. The French devaluations of 1982–3 (coming after a period of major policy errors) stand out as success stories (see Sachs and Wyplosz (1986)). Similarly, the Danish devaluation of 1982 was quite successful in re-establishing external equilibrium without significant costs in terms of unemployment (see De Grauwe and Vanhaverbeke (1990)).

2.2. *Devaluations to correct for supply shocks*

The preceding analysis can also be applied to the situation where one country experiences cost and price increases as a result of a supply shock. We show the dynamics of the

BOX 3   THE DEVALUATION OF THE BELGIAN FRANC OF 1982

In 1982 Belgium devalued its currency by 8.5%. In addition, fiscal and monetary policies were tightened, and an incomes policy. including temporary abolition of the wage–indexing mechanism, was instituted. This decision came after a period of several speculative crises during which the BF was put under severe pressures. These crises were themselves triggered by the increasing loss of competitiveness (in turn due to excessive wage increases) which the Belgian economy experienced during the 1970s. This has led to unsustainable current account deficits.

It can now be said that the devaluation (together with the other policy measures) was a great success. Not only did it lead to a rapid turnaround in the current account of the balance of payments (see Table B3.1). It managed to do so without imposing great deflationary pressures on the Belgian economy. As Table B3.2 shows, there was a pronounced recovery in employment after 1983. This recovery in employment proceeded at a pace that was not significantly different from the rest of the Community after that date.

Table B3.1 *Current account of Belgium (as a per cent of GDP)*

1981	−3.8
1982	−3.6
1983	−0.6
1984	−0.4
1985	0.5
1986	2.0

Source: EC Commission (1990).

Table B3.2. *Growth rate of employment (Belgium and EC)*

	Belgium	EC
1981	−2.0	−1.2
1982	−1.3	−0.9
1983	−1.1	−0.7
1984	0.0	0.1
1985	0.8	0.6
1986	1.0	0.8

Source: EC Commission (1990).

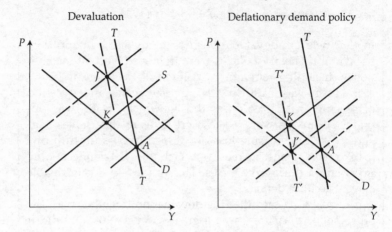

FIG. 2.5 Policy responses to supply shock

adjustment process in Fig. 2.5. The country is initially at point *A* and is hit by a negative supply shock, say a wage explosion of the type France experienced during the famous 'events of 1968'. This moves the economy to *K*, where we have a current account deficit and a general loss of competitiveness. With a devaluation, the aggregate demand curve shifts upwards and so does the aggregate supply curve. The economy settles at the new equilibrium point *J*. This is no improvement in terms of output compared to point *K*. Thus, the devaluation does not solve the real consequences of the negative supply shock. It does help, however, to improve the current account.

The policy of expenditure reduction has the same long-run consequences on output if prices and wages are flexible as a policy of devaluation. We show this in the right-hand panel of Fig. 2.5. The expenditure-reducing policy shifts the *TT*-line to the left. It also reduces aggregate demand for domestic goods. If, in addition, wages and prices are flexible, the supply curve shifts downwards. The new long-run equilibrium point is at *J'*. During the transition, however, the economy will experience a decline in output.

Here also the conclusion is that a devaluation cannot in the long run undo the supply shock. In this sense money is neutral in the long run. A devaluation can, however, be used to change the dynamics of the adjustment, making the latter less costly in terms of lost output and employment during the transition period towards long-run equilibrium.

3. Devaluation, Time Consistency, and Credibility

The idea that when the government follows particular policies it plays a game with the private sector has conquered macro-economic theory since the publication of the path-breaking articles of Kydland and Prescott (1977) and Barro–Gordon (1983).[10] This literature stresses that economic agents follow optimal strategies in response to the strategies of the authorities, and that these private sector responses have profound influences on the effectiveness of government policies. In particular, the reputation governments acquire in pursuing announced policies has a great impact on how these policies are going to affect the economy.

This literature also has important implications for our discussion of the costs of a monetary union. It leads to a fundamental criticism of the view that the exchange rate is a policy tool that governments have at their disposal to be used in a discretionary way. In order to understand this criticism it will be useful to present first the Barro–Gordon model for a closed economy, and then to apply it to an open economy, and to the choice of countries whether or not to join a monetary union.

3.1. The Barro–Gordon model: a geometric interpretation

Let us start from the standard Phillips curve which takes into account the role of inflationary expectations. We specify this Phillips curve as follows:

$$U = U_N + a(\dot{p}^e - \dot{p}) \tag{10}$$

where U is the unemployment rate, U_N is the natural unemployment rate, $\dot{p}$ is the observed rate of inflation, and $\dot{p}^e$ is the expected rate of inflation.

Equation (10) expresses the idea that only unexpected inflation affects the unemployment rate. Thus, when the

---

[10] The Barro–Gordon model has been applied to open economies by Mélitz (1988) and Cohen and Wyplosz (1989) among others.

inflation rate $\dot{p}$ is higher than the expected rate of inflation, the unemployment rate declines below its natural level.

We will also use the rational expectations assumption. This implies that economic agents use all relevant information to forecast the rate of inflation, and that they cannot be systematically wrong in making these forecasts. Thus, *on average* $\dot{p} = \dot{p}^{e}$, so that *on average* $U = U_{N}$.

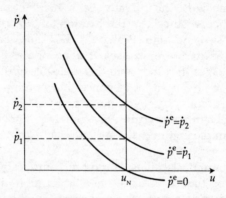

FIG. 2.6 The Phillips curve and natural unemployment

We represent the Phillips curve in Fig. 2.6.[11] The vertical line represents the 'long-term' vertical Phillips curve. It is the collection of all points for which $\dot{p} = \dot{p}^{e}$. This vertical line defines the natural rate of unemployment U_{N} which is also called the NAIRU (the non-accelerating-inflation rate of unemployment).

The second step in the analysis consists in introducing the preferences of the monetary authorities. The latter are assumed to care about both inflation and unemployment.

We represent these preferences in Fig. 2.7 in the form of a map of indifference curves of the authorities. We have drawn the indifference curves concave, expressing the idea that as the inflation rate declines, the authorities become less willing to let unemployment increase in order to reduce the inflation rate. Put differently, as the inflation rate declines the authorities tend

---

[11] Note that we set the inflation rate on the vertical axis. This contrasts with the representation used in sect. 2 of Ch. 1, where we had the rate of wage inflation on the vertical axis. We can, however, easily go from one representation to the other, considering that $w = p + q$, where we assume that the rate of productivity growth, q, is a constant.

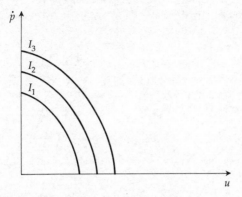

FIG. 2.7 The preferences of the authorities

to attach more weight to unemployment. Note also that the indifference curves closer to the origin represent a lower loss of welfare, and are thus preferred to those farther away from the origin.

The slope of these indifference curves expresses the relative importance the authorities attach to combating inflation or unemployment. In general, authorities who care much about unemployment ('wet' governments) have steep indifference curves, i.e. in order to reduce the rate of unemployment by one percentage point, they are willing to accept a lot of additional inflation.

On the other hand, 'hard-nosed' monetary authorities are willing to let the unemployment rate increase a lot in order to reduce the inflation rate by one percentage point. They have flat indifference curves. At the extreme, authorities who care only about inflation have horizontal indifference curves. We represent a few of these cases in Fig. 2.8.

We can now bring together the preferences of the authorities and the Phillips curves to determine the equilibrium of the model. We do this in Fig. 2.9.

In order to find out where the equilibrium will be located, assume for a moment that the government announces that it will follow a monetary policy rule of keeping the inflation rate equal to zero. Suppose also that the economic agents believe this announcement. They therefore set their expectations for

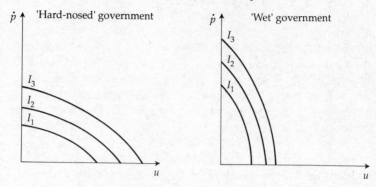

FIG. 2.8 The preferences of the authorities

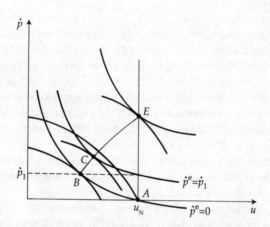

FIG. 2.9 The equilibrium inflation rate

inflation equal to zero. If the government implements this rule we move to point A.

It is now clear that the government can do better than point A. It could cheat and increase the rate of inflation unexpectedly. Thus, suppose that after having announced a zero inflation, the authorities increase the inflation rate unexpectedly. This would bring the economy to point B, which is located on a lower indifference curve. One can say that the government has an incentive to renege on its promise to maintain a zero inflation rate.

Will the government succumb to this temptation to engineer a surprise inflation? Not necessarily. The government also knows that economic agents are likely to react by increasing their expectations of inflation. Thus, during the next period, the Phillips curve is likely to shift upwards if the government decides to increase the rate of inflation unexpectedly. The government should therefore evaluate the short-term gain from cheating against the future losses that result from the fact that the Phillips curve shifts upwards.

But suppose now that the government consists of short-sighted politicians who give a low weight to future losses, and that it decides to cheat. We then move to point B. This, however, will trigger a shift of the Phillips curve upwards. Given these new expectations, it will be optimal for the authorities to move to point C. This will go on until we reach point E. This point has the following characteristics. First, it is on the vertical Phillips curve, so that agents' expectations are realized. They have therefore no incentives any more to change their expectations further. Secondly, at E the authorities have no incentive any more to surprise economic agents with more inflation. A movement upwards along the Phillips curve going through E would lead to an indifference curve located higher, and therefore to a loss of welfare.

Point E can also be interpreted as the equilibrium that will be achieved in a rational expectations world when the authorities follow a *discretionary* policy, i.e. when they set the rate of inflation optimally each period given the prevailing expectations.

It is clear that this equilibrium is not very attractive. It is however the only equilibrium that can be sustained, given that the authorities are sufficiently short-sighted, and that the private sector knows this. The zero inflation rule (or any other constant inflation rule below the level achieved at E) has no credibility in a world of rational economic agents. The reason is that these economic agents realize that the authorities have an incentive to cheat. They will therefore adjust their expectations up to the point where the authorities have no incentive to cheat any more. This is achieved at point E. A zero inflation rule, although desirable, will not come about automatically.[12]

[12] In the jargon of the economic literature it is said that the policy rule of zero inflation is 'time inconsistent', i.e. the authorities face the problem each period

It should be stressed that this model is a static one. If the policy game is repeated many times, the government will have an incentive to acquire a reputation of low inflation. Such a reputation will make it possible to reach a lower inflation equilibrium. One way the static assumption can be rationalized is by considering that in many countries political institutions favour short-term objectives for politicians. For example, the next election is never far away, leading to uncertainty whether the present rulers will still be in place next period. Thus, what is implicitly assumed in this model is that the political decision process is inefficient, leading politicians to give a strong weight to the short-term gains of inflationary policies. The politicians as individuals are certainly as rational as private agents; the political decision process, however, may force them to give undue weight to the very short-term results of their policies.

Before analysing the question of how a monetary union might help the authorities to move to a more attractive equilibrium, it is helpful to study what factors determine the exact location of the 'discretionary' equilibrium (point E).

We distinguish two factors that affect the location of the discretionary equilibrium, and therefore also the equilibrium level of inflation.

(a) The preferences of the authorities. In Fig. 2.10 we present the cases of the 'wet' (steep indifference curves) and the 'hard-nosed' (flat indifference curves) governments. Assuming that the Phillips curves have the same slopes, Fig. 2.10 shows that in a country with a 'wet' government, the equilibrium inflation will be higher than in the country with a 'hard-nosed' government.

Note also that the only way a zero rate of inflation rule can be credible is when the authorities show no concern whatsoever for unemployment. In that case the indifference curves are horizontal. The authorities will choose the lowest possible horizontal indifference curve in each period. The inflation equilibrium will then be achieved at point A.[13]

that a better short-term outcome is possible. The zero inflation rule is incentive-incompatible.

[13] Rogoff (1985) has suggested that the best thing that could happen to a country is that its monetary policy be run by an orthodox central banker.

The Theory of Optimum Currency Areas 51

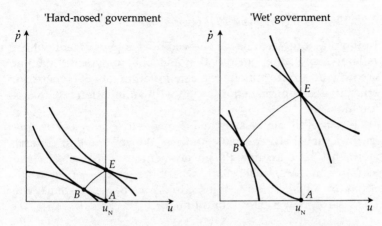

'Hard-nosed' government   'Wet' government

FIG. 2.10 Equilibrium with 'hard-nosed' and 'wet' governments

(b) The level of the natural rate of unemployment. Suppose the level of the natural unemployment rate increases. It can then easily be shown that if the preferences of the authorities remain unchanged, the new equilibrium inflation rate increases. This is made clear in Fig. 2.11 which shows the case of an increase of the NAIRU. Its effect is to increase the equilibrium rate of inflation from p to p'.

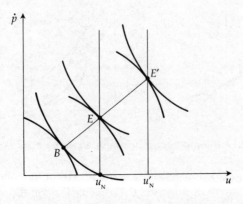

FIG. 2.11 Equilibrium and the level of natural unemployment

3.2. The Barro–Gordon model in open economies

In the previous sections we showed how a government, which is known to care about inflation and unemployment, will not credibly be able to announce a zero inflation rate. It is therefore stuck in a suboptimal equilibrium with an inflation rate that is too high.

This analysis can be extended to open economies. Let us now assume that there are two countries. We call the first country Germany, and assume its government is 'hard-nosed'. The second country is called Italy, where the government is 'wet'. As in the model presented in section 2 of Chapter 1, we use the purchasing-power parity condition, i.e.

$$\dot{e} = \dot{p}_I - \dot{p}_G$$

We show the inflation outcome in Fig. 2.12. Italy has a higher equilibrium rate of inflation than Germany. Its currency will therefore have to depreciate continuously. The problem of Italy is that it could achieve a much lower inflation equilibrium than point E if its government were able to convince its citizens that, once at point A, it would not try to reach point B.

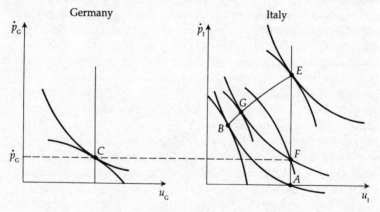

FIG. 2.12 Inflation equilibrium in a two-country model

This Barro–Gordon model for open economies allows us to add important insights into the discussion of the costs of a monetary union.

3.3. Credibility and the cost of a monetary union

Can Italy solve its problem by announcing that it will join a monetary union with Germany? In order to answer this question, suppose, first, that Italy announces that it will fix its exchange rate with the German mark. Given the purchasing-power parity, this fixes the Italian inflation rate at the German level. In Fig. 2.12 we show this by the horizontal line from *C*. Italy appears now to be able to enjoy a lower inflation rate. The potential welfare gains are large, because in the new equilibrium the economy is on a lower indifference curve.

The question, however, is whether this rule can be credible. We observe that once at the new equilibrium point *F*, the Italian authorities have an incentive to engineer a surprise devaluation of the lira. This surprise devaluation leads to a surprise increase in inflation and allows the economy to move towards point *G*. Over time, however, economic agents will adjust their expectations, so that the equilibrium inflation rate ends up to be the same as before the exchange rate was fixed. Thus, merely fixing the exchange rate does not solve the problem, because the fixed exchange rate rule is no more credible than a fixed inflation rate rule.[14]

There are, however, other arrangements that can potentially solve the high-inflation problem of Italy. Imagine that Italy decided to abolish its currency and to adopt the currency of Germany. If that arrangement could be made credible, i.e. if the Italian citizens were convinced that once this decision is taken and the mark becomes the national money, the Italian authorities would never rescind this decision, then Italy could achieve the same inflation equilibrium as Germany. In Fig. 2.12 the horizontal line connecting the German inflation equilibrium with Italy defines a credible equilibrium for Italy. The point *F* is now the new Italian inflation equilibrium. Since Italy has no independent monetary policy any more, its monetary authorities (with 'wet' preferences) have ceased to exist and therefore cannot devalue the lira. In the words of Giavazzi and Pagano

---

[14] We will come back to this issue when we discuss the workings of the EMS. Some economists have argued that fixing the exchange rate can be a rule that inherently has more credibility than announcing a constant inflation rate rule.

(1987), Italy has borrowed credibility from Germany, because its government has its monetary hands firmly tied.[15]

This is certainly a very strong result. It leads to the conclusion that there is a large potential gain for Italy in joining a monetary union with Germany. In addition, there is no welfare loss for Germany. Thus, a monetary union only leads to gains. This analysis has become very popular especially in Latin countries where the distrust for one's own authorities runs very deeply.

There are two considerations, however, that tend to soften this conclusion. First, it should be clear from the previous analysis that only a full monetary union establishes the required credibility for Italy. That is, Italy must be willing to eliminate its national currency, very much like East Germany did on 1 July 1990 when it adopted the West German mark. Anything less than full monetary union will face a credibility problem. As was pointed out, when Italy fixes its exchange rate relative to the mark and keeps its own currency, as it does in the EMS, the credibility of this fixed exchange rate arrangement will be in doubt. We return to this question when we analyse the workings of the European Monetary System.

Secondly, and more importantly for our present purpose, we have assumed that the central bank of the monetary union is the German central bank. In this arrangement, Italy profits from the reputation of the German central bank to achieve lower inflation. Suppose, however, that the new central bank is a new institution, where both the German and the Italian authorities are represented equally. Would that new central bank have the same reputation as the old German central bank? This is far from clear. If the union central bank is perceived to be less 'hard-nosed' than the German central bank prior to setting up the union, the new inflation equilibrium of the union will be higher than the one which prevailed in Germany before the union. Italy may still gain from such an arrangement. Germany, however, would lose, and would not be very enthusiastic to form such a union. We return to these issues in Chapter 8 where we discuss problems of setting up a European central bank, and of devising institutions that will enhance the low-inflation reputation of the European central bank.

---

[15] See also Giavazzi and Giovannini (1989).

We conclude from the preceding analysis that problems of credibility are important in evaluating the costs of a monetary union. First, the option to devalue the currency is a two-edged sword for the national authorities. The knowledge that it may be used in the future greatly complicates macroeconomic policies. Secondly, the time-consistency literature also teaches us some important lessons concerning the costs of a monetary union: a devaluation cannot be used to correct every disturbance that occurs in an economy. A devaluation is not, as it is in the analysis of Mundell, a flexible instrument that can be used frequently. When used once, it affects its use in the future, because it engenders strong expectational effects. It is a dangerous instrument that can hurt those who use it. Each time the policy-makers use this instrument, they will have to evaluate the advantages obtained today against the cost, i.e. that it will be more difficult to use this instrument effectively in the future.

This has led some economists to conclude that the exchange rate instrument should not be used at all, and that countries would even gain from irrevocably relinquishing its use. This conclusion goes too far. There were many cases, observed in Europe during the 1980s, in which devaluations were used very successfully (see the previous section). The ingredients of this success have typically been that the devaluation was coupled with other drastic policy changes (sometimes with a change of government, e.g. Belgium in 1982 and Denmark in the same year). As a result, the devaluation was perceived as a unique and an extraordinary change in policies that could not easily be repeated in the future. Under those conditions the negative reputation effects could be kept under control. Some countries, in particular Denmark in 1982, even seem to have improved their reputation quickly after the devaluation. Relinquishing the possibility of using this instrument for the indefinite future does imply a cost for a nation.

4. The Cost of Monetary Union and the Openness of Countries

Although it will remain difficult to evaluate the importance of all the arguments developed in the previous sections, and therefore of the costs of relinquishing one's national currency, we have learned one thing about which there can be relatively little dispute. The cost of relinquishing one's national currency declines with the openness of a country. This relation between the cost of joining a monetary union and the openness of the country was implicit in much of our previous analysis. Let us make it more explicit here.

The ability of a country to affect output and employment by exchange rate changes is certainly a function of its openness. Let us return to Fig. 2.3 where we analysed the effects of a devaluation. We now consider two countries, one that is relatively open, the other that is relatively closed. We represent these two countries in Fig. 2.13.

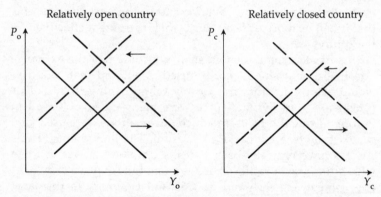

Relatively open country   Relatively closed country

FIG. 2.13 Effectiveness of devaluation as a function of openness

The major difference between open and relatively closed countries has to do with the supply shifts that follow a devaluation. More than a relatively closed country, a very open economy will quickly be faced with the problem that a devaluation just raises the domestic price level without affecting its output. Thus, for a very open economy the exchange rate is a particularly ineffective instrument. Relinquishing this instrument, therefore, involves little loss.

McKinnon (1963) has stressed this point in his important contribution to the theory of optimum currency areas. When the country is very open, economic agents (workers and employers) may start using the foreign price level when setting contracts. In that case, changing the exchange rate would be completely redundant, because these economic agents would automatically adjust the domestic currency value of all these contracts. The country could take over the foreign currency without any loss.

In addition, for small open economies the alternative instruments needed to bring back equilibrium in the balance of payments are less likely to impose the same kind of large costs as for relatively closed countries. This can be illustrated by considering the following simple Keynesian model of aggregate demand in small and large economies. Let us define a very open country as one with a high marginal propensity to import, and a relatively closed country as one with a low marginal propensity to import. The multiplier of government spending can then be derived for the two countries to be the following:

for the open economy

$$Y = \frac{1}{s + m} G$$

for the relatively closed country

$$Y^* = \frac{1}{s^* + m^*} G^*$$

where G and G^* are the levels of government spending in the two countries, s and s^* are the marginal propensities to save, and m and m^* are the marginal propensities to import in the two countries.

Suppose both countries use government spending as their instrument to reduce the deficit on the trade account. The effect of reducing government spending on the trade account is then described by the following equations:

for the open economy

$$B = \frac{m}{s + m} G$$

for the relatively closed country

$$B^* = \frac{m^*}{s^* + m^*} G^*$$

where B and B^* are the trade accounts of the open and the relatively closed countries.

It can be seen from these expressions that to obtain the same effect on its trade account the more open economy will have to reduce government spending more than the relatively closed country. An example makes this clear. Suppose the marginal propensity to import is 0.5 in the first country and 0.1 in the second one. Let us also assume that the marginal propensities to save are equal to 0.2 in both countries. Then the multipliers of government spending on the trade account are 0.71 and 0.33, respectively. This implies that if the objective is to reduce the trade account by 100 the relatively closed economy will have to reduce government spending by 300 whereas the relatively open economy achieves the same reduction of its trade account by reducing government spending by 140. Thus, reducing the trade account by general fiscal policies will be less costly for the relatively open economy than for the relatively closed one.

We can summarize these ideas about the costs of a monetary union and the openness of the country in Fig. 2.14 (which is borrowed from Krugman (1990)). On the vertical axis the cost of a monetary union is set out (i.e. the cost of relinquishing the exchange rate instrument). This cost is expressed as a per cent of GDP. On the horizontal axis the openness of the country relative to the countries with whom it wants to form a monetary union is set out. This openness is represented by the trade

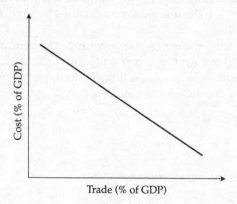

FIG. 2.14 The cost of a monetary union and the openness of a country

share in the GDP of the country considered here. We see that as the openness increases the cost of joining a monetary union declines.

5. Conclusion

The criticism against the traditional theory of optimal currency areas, as developed by Mundell and McKinnon, has enabled us to add important nuances to this theory. In particular, it has changed our view about the costs of a monetary union. The traditional theory of optimal currency areas tends to be rather pessimistic about the possibility for countries to join a monetary union at a low cost. The criticism we have discussed in this chapter is much less pessimistic about this, i.e. the costs of forming a monetary union appear to be less forbidding. Despite this criticism the hard core of the optimum currency analysis still stands. This can be put as follows:

1. There are important differences between countries that are not going to disappear in a monetary union. This raises the question whether countries should gladly relinquish control over their ability to follow an independent monetary policy, including setting (and changing) the price of their currency.
2. Despite the fact that exchange rate changes usually have no permanent effects on real variables, such as output and employment, variations in the exchange rate remain a powerful instrument to help countries to eliminate important macroeconomic disequilibria, and to make the adjustment process less costly in terms of lost output and employment. The examples of France, Belgium, and Denmark that devalued their currencies during the 1980s (and coupled this devaluation with the right domestic policies) illustrate this point.
3. The argument that exchange rate changes ~~ ~~ dangerous instruments in the hands of politicians is experience of many countries illustrates that wh are used systematically, they will lead to more gains in terms of output and employment. easily lead to macroeconomic instability as continuously tend to expect future devaluat

the old view, devaluations are not instruments that policy-makers can use flexibly and costlessly.

This argument should, however, not be pushed too far. The fact that such an instrument can be misused is not sufficient reason to throw it away, when it can also be put to good use, when countries face extraordinary circumstances. The abandonment of the exchange rate instrument to deal with possible extraordinary disturbances should certainly be considered to be a cost of monetary union.

3

The Benefits of a Common Currency

Introduction

Whereas the costs of a common currency have much to do with the *macroeconomic* management of the economy, the benefits are mostly situated at the *microeconomic* level. Eliminating national currencies and moving to a common currency can be expected to lead to gains in economic efficiency. These gains in efficiency have two different origins. One is the elimination of transaction costs associated with the exchanging of national moneys. The other is the elimination of risk coming from the uncertain future movements of the exchange rates. In this chapter we analyse these two sources of benefits of a monetary union.

1. Direct Gains from the Elimination of Transaction Costs

Eliminating the costs of exchanging one currency into the other is certainly the most visible (and most easily quantifiable) gain from a monetary union. We have all experienced these costs whenever we exchanged one currency for another. These costs disappear when countries move to a common European currency.

How large are these gains from the elimination of transaction costs? The EC Commission has recently estimated these gains, and arrives at a number between 13 to 20 billion ECUs per year.[1] This represents one-quarter to one-half of one per cent of

---

[1] See EC Commission (1990).

the Community GDP. This may seem peanuts. It is, however, a gain that has to be added to the other gains from a single market.

It should be noted here that these gains that accrue to the general public have a counterpart somewhere. They are mostly to be found in the banking sector. Surveys in different countries indicate that about 5% of the banks' revenues are the commissions paid to banks in the exchange of national currencies. This source of revenue for the banks will disappear with a monetary union.

The preceding should not give the impression that the gain for the public is offset by the loss of the banks. The transaction costs involved in exchanging money are a *deadweight* loss. They are like a tax paid by the consumer in exchange for which he gets nothing. Banks, however, will have a problem of transition: they will have to look for other profitable activities. When this has been done, society will have gained. The banks' employees, previously engaged in exchanging money, will now be free to perform more useful tasks for society.

Another point to be made here is that the gains from the elimination of transaction costs can only be reaped when national moneys are replaced by a common currency. These gains are unlikely to occur if in a future monetary union national moneys would remain in place, albeit with irrevocably fixed exchange rates. There are several reasons for this conclusion.

First, as long as national currencies remain in existence, even if the exchange rate is 'irrevocably' fixed, doubts will continue to exist as to this fixity. This will stimulate residents of each country to use their home currency in preference to foreign ones. In other words, currencies will not be perfect substitutes. There will continue to be a need to convert one currency into another. Those that provide this service will charge a price (a difference between the bid and ask rates). Transaction costs will not be eliminated.

These transaction costs are likely to remain as high as they are today. We have some evidence for this conclusion from the fact that the difference between bid and ask rates is not very sensitive to the degree of exchange rate fluctuations. We present some evidence of this in Table 3.1. (For more systematic evidence confirming that the bid–ask spread is not very

TABLE 3.1 *Bid–Ask spreads of the Belgian franc against some major currencies (%, 21 December 1990)*

German mark	0.48
French franc	0.49
Guilder	0.49
Pound sterling	0.54
US dollar	0.57

Source: Computed from *De Financieel Economische Tijd*, 22 Dec. 1990.

sensitive to the degree of exchange rate variability, see Boyd, Gielens, and Gros (1990).) We observe that despite the fact that there have been no major changes between the Belgian franc, the guilder, and the German mark for several years, the bid–ask spread (and thus the cost of transacting these currencies) is barely lower than the bid–ask spread between the Belgian franc and the dollar (or the pound sterling), two currencies that have fluctuated wildly against the Belgian franc. This evidence suggests that the reduction of exchange rate variability between the Belgian franc, the guilder, and the German mark has not reduced the transaction costs significantly. These transaction costs can only be eliminated if a common currency is introduced. (We return to this difference between a common currency and fixed exchange rates in Chapter 6.)

2. Indirect Gains from Eliminating Transaction Costs

The elimination of transaction costs will also have an indirect (albeit less easily quantifiable) gain. It will reduce the scope for price discrimination between national markets.

There is a lot of evidence that price discrimination is still practised widely in Europe. (See EC Commission (1988) for evidence.) In Table 3.2 we illustrate this phenomenon in the automobile market. It can be seen that in the UK the same automobiles were about 60% more expensive than in Denmark and 30% more expensive than in Belgium (net of taxes). There is also evidence that these differentials have not declined during the 1980s.

Such price discrimination is only possible because national markets are still segmented. That is, there are relatively large transaction costs for the consumer who would buy a car in another country. If these transaction costs did not exist, consumers would not hesitate to purchase these goods in the countries where they are cheap. Of course, there are many sources of transaction costs (e.g. administrative regulations, differences in taxation), and eliminating the cost of buying and selling foreign currencies may not even be the most important one. However, together with the other measures to create a single market, they would make price discrimination much more difficult. This would be a benefit for the European consumer.

3. Welfare Gains from Less Uncertainty

The uncertainty about future exchange rate changes introduces uncertainty about future revenues of firms. It is generally accepted that this leads to a loss of welfare in a world populated by risk-averse individuals. These will, generally speaking, prefer a future return that is more certain than one that is less so, at least if the expected value of these returns is the same. Put

TABLE 3.2 *Average price differentials (net of taxes) for the same automobile in Europe, 1986 and 1989 (Denmark = 100)*

	1986	1989
Belgium	121	123
Denmark	100	100
France	130	132
Germany	129	137
Italy	144	148
Netherlands	123	130
UK	151	161

Source: N. Van Neder and W. Vanhaverbeke (1990).

differently, they will only want to take the more risky return if they are promised that it will be higher than the less risky. Eliminating the exchange risk reduces a source of uncertainty and should therefore increase welfare.

There is one important feature of the theory of the firm that may invalidate that conclusion. Take a profit-maximizing firm which is a price-taker in the output market. We represent its marginal cost curve and the price of its output in Fig. 3.1. Suppose there are two regimes. In the first regime (presented in the left-hand panel) the price is constant and perfectly predictable by the firm. In the second regime (right-hand panel) the price fluctuates randomly. We assume here that the price fluctuates symmetrically between p_2 and p_3.

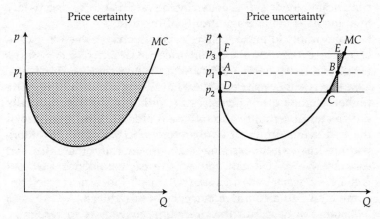

FIG. 3.1 Profits of the firm under price certainty and uncertainty

In the first regime of certainty the profit of the firm in each period is given by the shaded area. In the second uncertain regime the profit will fluctuate depending on whether the price p_2 or p_3 prevails. We can now see that the profit will be larger on average in the uncertain regime than in the certain regime. When the price is low the profit is lower than in the certainty case by the area $ABCD$. When the price is high, the profit is higher than the certainty case by the area $FEBA$. It can now easily be seen that $FEBA$ is larger than $ABCD$. The difference is given by the two darkened triangles.

This result has the following interpretation. When the price is high the firm increases output so as to profit from the higher revenue per unit of output. Thus, it gains a higher profit for each unit of output it would have produced anyway, and *in addition* it expands its output. The latter effect is measured by the upper darkened triangle. When the price is low, however, the firm will do the opposite, it will reduce output. In so doing it limits the reduction in its total profit. This effect is represented by the lower darkened triangle.

There are many complications that can be added to this theory. For example, one can introduce the assumption of imperfect competition, or the assumption that there are adjustment costs. In general, the conclusions may not be as sharp as in the simple case presented here. Nevertheless, in these more complicated models, it is generally the case that price uncertainty may increase the average profits of the firm.

If one wants to make welfare comparisons between a regime of price certainty and one of price uncertainty, the positive effect of price uncertainty on the average profits should be compared to the greater uncertainty about these profits. The higher average profit increases the utility of the firm, whereas the greater uncertainty about these profits reduces the utility of the (risk-averse) firm. It is, therefore, unclear whether welfare will decline when exchange rate uncertainty increases, or, conversely that we can say with great confidence that the welfare of firms will increase when national currencies are eliminated and a common currency is introduced.

Another way to put the preceding analysis is to recognize that changes in the exchange rate do not only represent a risk, they also create opportunities to make profits. When the exchange rate becomes more variable the probability of making very large profits increases. In a certain sense, exporting can be seen as an *option*. When the exchange rate becomes very favourable the firm exercises its option to export. With an unfavourable exchange rate the firm does not exercise this option. It is well known from option theory that the value of the option increases when the variability of the underlying asset increases. Thus, the firm that has the option to export is better off when the exchange rate becomes more variable.

The same argument can be developed for the *consumer*. In Fig.

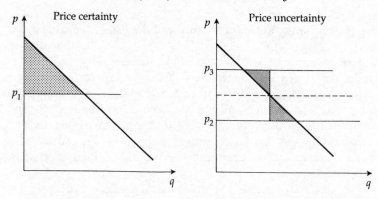

F ig. 3.2 Average consumer surplus and price volatility

3.2 we present the demand function of a representative consumer. Suppose again that there are two regimes of price volatility. In the first regime the price is constant and perfectly predictable. In the second regime the price fluctuates randomly between p_2 and p_3. We find that in the second regime of price uncertainty the consumer surplus is higher on average than in the first regime of price certainty. The reason is the same as in the case of the firm. When the price is low, the consumer increases his demand to profit from the low price. When the price is high he does the opposite, and thereby limits the negative effect the price increase has on his welfare. Thus, on average, the consumer gains when prices fluctuate.

This positive effect of price uncertainty on the average consumer surplus has to be compared to the increased risk. To the extent that consumers are risk-averse they will give a lower utility value to the higher (but uncertain) consumer surplus than to the lower consumer surplus obtained in a regime of certainty. Our conclusion from the static theory of the consumer is that we do not know whether consumers gain from lower price variability. We also conclude that if gains from a common currency and the ensuing reduction in risk are to be expected, they should probably be found elsewhere than in the static welfare gains that we have analysed in this section.

4. Exchange Rate Uncertainty and the Price Mechanism

There is another area where more substantial gains from a reduction of the exchange rate risk can be expected. Exchange rate uncertainty introduces uncertainty about the future prices of goods and services. Economic agents base their decisions concerning production, investment, and consumption on the information that the price system provides for them. If these prices become more uncertain the quality of these decisions will decline.

We can make these general statements more concrete by considering an example. Suppose a firm decides to invest in a foreign country. It bases this decision on many variables. One of these is the expected future exchange rate. Suppose then that after having made the investment, it turns out that the exchange rate on which the decision was made was wrong and that this forecast error makes the whole investment unprofitable so that the firm decides to close its foreign operation. Such errors will be costly. One can also expect them to be more frequent when uncertainty about the future exchange rate increases. In this sense, the price system, which gives signals to individuals to produce or to invest, becomes less reliable as a mechanism to allocate resources.

It should be stressed that the exchange rate uncertainty discussed here has to do with *real* exchange rate uncertainty. That is, the uncertainty comes about because the exchange rate changes do not reflect price changes. A well-known example is the dollar appreciation during 1980–85 which was largely unpredicted and which went much farther than the inflation differential between the US and the other industrial countries. In other words, the dollar deviated substantially from its purchasing power parity. This 'misalignment' led to large and unpredicted changes in the profitability of many American industrial firms which had to compete in world markets. It also led to declines in output and firm closures. A few years later the dollar depreciated substantially and more than corrected the real appreciation of the first half of the 1980s. These large real exchange rate movements led to large adjustment costs for the

American economy. (For a well-known analysis of the effects of misalignment see Williamson (1983).)

A decline in real exchange rate uncertainty, due for example to the introduction of a common currency, can reduce these adjustment costs. As a result, the price system becomes a better guide to make the right economic decisions. These efficiency gains are difficult to quantify. They are no less important for this. Their importance becomes all the more visible when we look at what happens in countries that experience hyperinflation. We observe in these countries that the wrong production and investment decisions are made on a massive scale. Quite often we observe that output and investment booms in countries with hyperinflation. However, these increases in output and investment frequently occur in the wrong sectors or product lines. After a while these productions and investments have to be abandoned. Massive amounts of resources are wasted in the process.

There is a second reason why greater price and exchange rate uncertainty may reduce the quality of the information provided by the price mechanism. An increase in risk, due to price uncertainty, will in general increase the real interest rate. This follows from the fact that when the expected return on investment projects becomes more uncertain, risk-averse investors will require a higher risk premium to compensate them for the increased riskiness of the projects. In addition, in a riskier economic environment, economic agents will increase the discount rate at which they discount future returns. Thus, exchange rate uncertainty which leads to this kind of increased systemic risk also increases the real interest rate. Higher interest rates, however, lead to increased problems in selecting investment projects in an efficient way. These problems have to do with *moral hazard* and *adverse selection*.

The *moral hazard problem* arises because an increase in the interest rate changes the incentives of the borrower. The latter will find it more advantageous to increase the riskiness of his investment projects. This follows from an asymmetry of expected profits and losses. If the investment project is successful the extra profits go to the borrower. If the investment project turns out badly and if the borrower goes bankrupt, his loss is limited to his equity share in the project. With a higher interest rate this moral hazard problem becomes more intense. This asymmetry gives the borrower the incentive to select more risky projects. Thus, on average investment projects will become riskier when the real interest rate increases. Lenders, however, will try to defend themselves by asking for an additional risk premium, which in turn intensifies the problem. In general, the moral hazard problem may lead the lender to apply credit ceilings as a way to reduce his risk.[2]

The *adverse selection problem* leads to a similar result. When the interest rate increases, the suppliers of low-risk investment projects will tend to drop out of the credit market. They will find it less attractive to borrow at the higher interest rate for projects that do not represent a high risk. Thus, on average, the riskiness of investment projects will increase when the interest rate increases.

Both phenomena, moral hazard and adverse selection, lead to the selection of more risky investment projects. Thus, the systemic risk increases. Eliminating that risk by moving towards a common currency reduces the amount of risky projects that are selected by the market.

We can conclude this section by noting that the movement towards a common currency will eliminate the exchange risk, and thereby will lead to a more efficient working of the price mechanism. Although this effect cannot easily be measured, it is likely to be an important benefit of the introduction of one currency in Europe.

It should be noted here that not all economists will share this conclusion. Some have argued that the elimination of the exchange risk can only be obtained by introducing more risk elsewhere in the economic system. As a result, we are not sure whether the systemic risk is reduced by eliminating just one source of risk. We return to this issue in Box 4 where we evaluate this argument.

---

[2] See the classic article of Stiglitz and Weiss (1981).

5. Exchange Rate Uncertainty and Economic Growth

The argument that the elimination of the exchange risk will lead to an increase in economic growth can be made using the neoclassical growth model, and its recent extension to situations of dynamic economies of scale. This analysis features prominently in the recent EC report 'One Market, One Money' (1990) which in turn was very much influenced by Baldwin (1989).

The neoclassical growth model is represented in Fig. 3.3. The horizontal axis shows the capital stock per worker, the vertical axis the output per worker. The line $f(k)$ is the production function which has the usual convex shape, implying diminishing marginal productivities. The equilibrium in this model is obtained where the marginal productivity of capital is equal to the interest rate consumers use to discount future consumption. This is represented in Fig. 3.3 by the point A, where the line rr (whose slope is equal to the discount rate) is tangent to the production function $f(k)$. In this model, growth can only occur if the population grows or if there is an exogenous rate of technological change. (Note also that in this neoclassical model the savings ratio does not influence the equilibrium growth rate.)

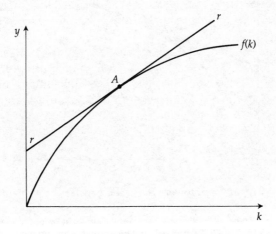

FIG. 3.3 The neoclassical growth model

We can now use this model as a starting-point to evaluate the growth effects of a monetary union. Assume that the elimination of the exchange risk reduces the systemic risk so that the real interest rate declines. We represent this effect in Fig. 3.4. The reduction of the risk-adjusted rate of discount makes the *rr*-line flatter. As a result, the equilibrium moves from *A* to *B*. There will be an accumulation of capital and an increase in the growth rate while the economy moves from *A* to *B*. In the new equilibrium, output per worker and the capital stock he has at his disposal will have increased. Note, however, that the growth rate of output then returns to its initial level, which is determined by the exogenous rate of technological change and the rate of growth of the population. Thus, in this neoclassical growth model the reduction of the interest rate due to the monetary union *temporarily* increases the rate of growth of output. In the new equilibrium the output *level* per worker will have increased. (Note also that the productivity of capital has declined.)

This model has recently been extended by introducing dynamic economies of scale.[3] Suppose the productivity of

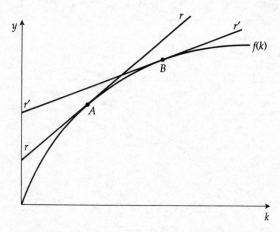

FIG. 3.4 The effect of lower risk in the neoclassical growth model

---

[3] See Romer (1986). What is new here is the formalization of old ideas. Many economists in the past have stressed that the growth phenomenon is based on dynamic economies of scale and learning effects.

capital increases when the capital stock increases. This may arise because with a higher capital stock and output per worker there are learning effects and additional knowledge is accumulated. This additional knowledge then increases the labour productivity in the next period. There may also be a public goods aspect to knowledge. Thus, once a new machine is in place the knowledge it embodies is freely available to the worker who uses it. All these effects produce increases in the productivity of labour over time when capital accumulates.

One of the interesting characteristics of these new growth models is that the growth path becomes endogenous, and is sensitive to the initial conditions. Thus, an economy that starts with a higher capital stock per worker can move on a permanently higher growth path.

A lowering of the interest rate can likewise put the economy on a permanently higher growth path. We represent this case in Fig. 3.5. As a result of the lower interest rate the economy accumulates more capital. Contrary to the static case of Fig. 3.4, however, this raises the productivity of the capital stock per worker. This is shown by the upward movement of the $f(k)$ line. The economy will be on a higher growth path.

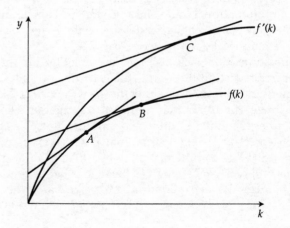

FIG. 3.5 Endogenous growth in the 'new' growth model

The previous analysis sounds very promising for the growth effects of a monetary union.[4] It is, however, most probably a little too optimistic, for it ignores the point that was made in section 3 above, that is, a reduction of exchange rate variability also reduces the expected value of future profits of firms. Thus, a lower risk due to less exchange rate variability has a double effect. It reduces the real interest rate (which in the previous analysis generated the growth effect) *and* it reduces the expected return of investment. As a result, this reduction in risk has an ambiguous effect on investment activity, and thus also on the growth of output.

This point is not generally recognized by the public. Quite often it is stated that a reduction of the risk will boost investment activity. Economic theory does not allow us to draw this conclusion. The question whether a reduction of the exchange risk increases investment, therefore, is an empirical one. What does the empirical evidence tell us?

There has been a large amount of empirical analysis of the relation between exchange rate uncertainty and international trade and investment. (For a survey, see IMF (1984).) On the whole it is fair to say that very little relation has been found. In other words, the increased variability of the exchange rates, and in particular the large and unpredictable variability of the real exchange rates, does not seem to have had very significant effects on international trade and investment. This implies that the link between exchange rate uncertainty and economic growth is empirically also a very weak one.

We illustrate this lack of empirical relationship between exchange rate variability and the growth of output and investment in Table 3.3. We show the growth rates of GDP and of investment in industrial countries during the 1980s. We classify these countries into two groups, those that have experienced relatively stable (nominal and real) exchange rates (mainly the EMS countries) and those that have seen their (nominal and real) exchange rates fluctuate a lot. In general, the latter countries have experienced exchange variability (both

---

[4] This analysis was also implicit in the hope of the founding fathers of the EMS that the greater exchange rate stability provided by the system would stimulate the growth of investment, output, and trade in Europe.

TABLE 3.3 *Growth of GDP and investment, 1981–1990*

	GDP	Investment
EMS countries		
Belgium	1.9	2.0
Denmark	1.9	1.3
Germany	2.1	1.7
France	2.1	1.8
Ireland	2.8	0.3
Italy	2.5	2.0
Netherlands	1.8	2.6
Non-EMS countries		
Portugal	2.7	4.2
Spain (until 1989)	2.7	5.3
UK	2.4	3.8
USA	3.0	3.6
Japan	4.1	5.9

Source: EC Commission (1990).

nominal and real) that is three to five times as large as the former.

The figures of Table 3.3 are striking. The greater exchange rate stability that the EMS countries have experienced during the 1980s does not seem to have provided a great boost to the growth rates of output and investment.[5] As a matter of fact, the growth rates of output and investment have on average been lower in the EMS countries than in the non-EMS countries that experienced relatively large movements in their exchange rates.

Another way to illustrate this lack of a robust relationship between economic growth and exchange rate risk is to look at the growth rate of countries as a function of their size. Large countries have a large monetary zone within which there is no exchange rate uncertainty. Firms in small countries typically

[5] For more evidence on the growth effects of the EMS see De Grauwe (1987). Note that it is not implied here that the greater exchange rate stability observed in the EMS has not been beneficial for the EMS countries. What is implied is that this greater exchange rate stability does not seem to have had much beneficial effect on the growth rates of output and investment.

face much more exchange rate uncertainty because they sell a larger proportion of their final output to countries in different monetary areas. Thus, a large part of these sales face exchange rate uncertainty. Therefore one would expect that if a reduction of exchange rate uncertainty stimulates economic growth, larger countries will on average experience a higher growth rate of output than small countries. We show some evidence in Fig. 3.6. On the vertical axis we present the growth rates during 1965–87, on the horizontal axis the size of these countries as measured by their GDP (in 1987). It is immediately clear that there is no relationship between the size of countries and their growth rates.

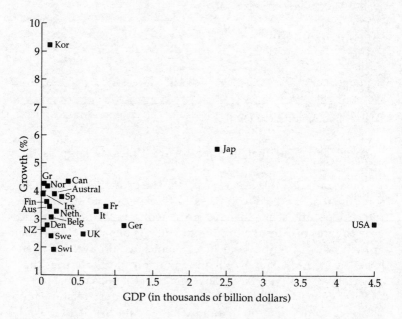

FIG. 3.6 Growth rates of GDP (1965–1987) and level of GDP (1987)
Source: World Bank, *World Development Report*, Washington, DC, 1991.

The previous evidence is of course only meant to be suggestive. Most of the many econometric studies that have been performed recently tend to confirm that the degree of exchange rate variability has a very weak impact on the growth rates of investment, trade, and output. Thus, the weakness of the theoretical argument for such a relationship is confirmed by a weakness of the empirical relationship.

There are, however, two other possible explanations for our failure to find a significant empirical relationship between exchange rate uncertainty and economic growth.

A first alternative explanation is that when we compare the experience of the EMS countries with the other countries, we fail to take into account the fact that the exchange rate uncertainty within the EMS, although reduced, has not been eliminated. It may be that the movement to full monetary union with a common currency is the step we need to eliminate the exchange rate uncertainty, and to stimulate economic growth. (Note, however, that this interpretation of the empirical results is less convincing when we look at the evidence concerning the size of countries.)

A second more promising explanation is that the reduction in exchange rate uncertainty may not necessarily reduce the systemic risk. Less exchange rate uncertainty may be compensated by greater uncertainty elsewhere, e.g. interest rate uncertainty. As a result, firms that face a greater monetary zone may not on average operate in a less risky environment. There is a whole theoretical literature, starting with William Poole (1970) that has analysed this problem. We have presented the main results in Box 4.

6. Benefits of a Monetary Union and the Openness of Countries

As in the chapter on the costs of a monetary union, we can also derive a relationship between the *benefits* of a monetary union and the openness of a country. The welfare gains of a monetary union that we have identified in this chapter are likely to increase with the degree of openness of an economy. For example, the elimination of transaction costs will weigh more heavily in countries where firms and consumers buy and sell a large fraction of goods and services in foreign countries. Similarly, the consumers and the firms in these countries are more subject to decision errors because they face large foreign

BOX 4   FIXING EXCHANGE RATES AND SYSTEMIC RISK

In a path-breaking article William Poole (1970) showed that fixing interest rates does not necessarily reduce the volatility of output compared to fixing the money stock. The argument Poole developed can easily be extended to the choice between fixed and flexible exchange rates.

Suppose we can represent the economy by the standard *IS–LM* model. In an open economy with perfect capital mobility the domestic interest rate is equal to the foreign interest rate plus the expected future depreciation of the domestic currency (open interest parity).

We consider first *random shocks occurring in the goods market* (business cycle shocks for example). We present this by shifts in the *IS* curve. The latter now moves unpredictably between IS_U and IS_L.

Let us assume first that the authorities fix the exchange rate, and that this fixed exchange rate is credible, so that the domestic interest rate must be equal to the foreign interest rate. We represent the model graphically in Fig. B4.1.

The flexibility of the exchange rate here implies that the domestic interest rate is constant (assuming no changes in the foreign interest rate). Thus, output will fluctuate between Y_L and Y_U. (Note that as the *IS* curve moves to, say, IS_U the *LM* curve will also automatically be displaced to the right, so that it intersects IS_U at the point F. This movement of the *LM* curve comes from the fact that the upward movement of the *IS* curve tends to increase the domestic interest rate: with perfect capital mobility this leads to capital inflows, which increase the domestic money stock.)

What happens if the authorities allow the exchange rate to be flexible, and instead fix the domestic money stock? In this case the *LM* curve remains fixed. The same shocks in the *LM* curve now lead to smaller disturbances in the output level. The range of fluctuation of domestic output is now given by the points Y'_L and Y'_U. The intuition behind this result can best be explained by an example. Suppose the *IS* curve shifts upwards (say due to a domestic boom). This tends to increase the domestic interest rate. Since the exchange rate is flexible, there can be no increase in the money stock from net capital inflows. Instead, the increase in the domestic interest rate leads to an appreciation of the currency. Thus the increase in the domestic interest rate and the appreciation dampen the domestic boom in economic activity.

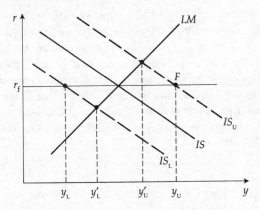

FIG. B4.1 Shocks in the *IS* curve

We conclude from this case that fixing the exchange rate has led to more variability in the output market compared to letting the exchange rate vary. Fixing the exchange rate does not reduce systemic risk, because it leads to more uncertainty elsewhere in the system. This result, however, very much depends on the nature of the random shocks, that were assumed to come from the goods markets. Things are quite different if the random shocks originate from the money market.

Suppose that we have *random disturbances in the demand for money* (disturbances in velocity). We represent these by movements in the *LM* curve between the limits LM_L and LM_U in Fig. B4.2. Let us again consider the case where the authorities fix the exchange rate. As before, this means that the domestic interest rate is fixed (assuming no shocks in the foreign interest rate). It can now immediately be established that there will be no change in output. The reason is the following. Suppose that the demand for money has declined leading to a rightward shift of the *LM* curve. This tends to reduce the interest rate. Such a reduction, however, is prevented by a capital outflow. At the same time the money stock declines. The *LM* curve must return to its initial level. Thus, the goods market is completely insulated from money market disturbances when the authorities fix the exchange rate.

If the authorities allow the exchange rate to float, this will not be the case any more. Output will now fluctuate between the levels Y_L' and Y_U'. The intuition is that if the *LM* curve shifts to the right, the ensuing decline in the interest rate leads to a depreciation of the currency, whereas the domestic money supply remains unchanged. The decline in the interest rate and the depreciation tend to stimulate aggregate demand. The goods market is not insulated from the money market disturbances.

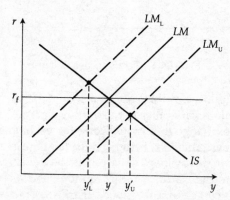

FIG. B4.2 Shocks in the *LM* curve

markets with different currencies. Eliminating these risks will lead to a larger welfare gain (per capita) in small and open economies than in large and relatively closed countries.

We can represent this relationship between the benefits of a monetary union and the openness of the countries that are candidates for a union graphically. This is done in Fig. 3.7. On the horizontal axis we show the openness of the country relative to its potential partners of the monetary union (measured

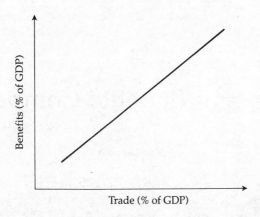

FIG. 3.7 Benefits of a monetary union and openness of the country

by the share of their bilateral trade in the GDP of the country considered). On the vertical axis we represent the benefits (as a percentage of GDP). With an increasing openness towards the other partners in the union, the gains from a monetary union (per unit of output) increase.

7. Conclusion

A common currency has important benefits. In this chapter several of these benefits were identified. First, a common currency in Europe will eliminate transaction costs. This will not only produce direct, but also indirect benefits in that it will make it more difficult for firms to apply price discrimination in Europe. Secondly, by reducing price uncertainty, a common currency will improve the allocative efficiency of the price mechanism. This will certainly improve welfare, although it is difficult to quantify this effect.

We have also concluded that we should not expect too much additional economic growth from a mone potential growth-boosting effects of a mon been oversold. The theoretical reasons for a r stimulate economic growth are weak, and s evidence. The benefits of a monetary unio elsewhere than in its alleged growth-stimul

4

Costs and Benefits Compared

Introduction

In the previous chapters the costs and benefits of a monetary union were identified. In this chapter we conclude this discussion by comparing the benefits with the costs in a synthetic way. This will allow us to draw some general conclusions about the economic desirability of joining a monetary union by individual European countries.

1. Costs and Benefits Compared

It is useful to combine the figures (derived in the previous chapters) relating benefits and costs to the openness of a country. This is done in Fig. 4.1. The intersection point of the benefit and the cost lines determines the critical level of openness that makes it worthwhile for a country to join a monetary union with its trading partners. To the left of that point, the country is better off keeping its national currency. To the right it is better off when it relinquishes its national money and replaces it with the money of its trading partners.

Fig. 4.1 allows us to draw some qualitative conclusions concerning the importance of costs and benefits. The shape and the position of the cost schedule depends to a large extent on one's view about the effectiveness of the exchange rate instrument in correcting for the effects of different demand and cost developments between the countries involved.

At one extreme, there is a view, which will be called 'monetarist', claiming that exchange rate changes are ineffective as instruments to correct for these different developments between countries. And even if they are effective, the use of xchange rate policies typically make countries worse off. In

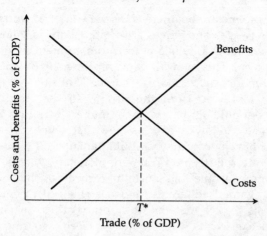

FIG. 4.1 Costs and benefits of a monetary union

this 'monetarist' view[1] the cost curve is very close to the origin. We represent this case in Fig. 4.2 (*a*). The critical point that makes it worthwhile to form a union is close to the origin. Thus, in this view, many countries in the world would gain by relinquishing their national currencies, and by joining a monetary union.

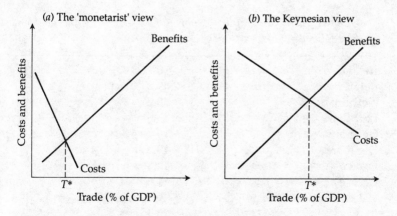

FIG. 4.2 Costs and benefits of a monetary union

[1] This is the view taken by the drafters of the recent EC Commission report (1990).

At the other extreme, there is the view that the world is full of rigidities (wages and prices are rigid, labour is immobile), so that the exchange rate is a powerful instrument in eliminating disequilibria. This view is well represented by the original Mundell model discussed in Chapter 1. In this view, the cost curve is far away from the origin, so that relatively few countries should find it in their interest to join a monetary union. It also follows from this view that many large countries that now have one currency would be better off (economically) splitting the country into different monetary zones.

It is unmistakable that since the early 1980s the 'monetarist' view has gained adherents, and has changed the view many economists have about the desirability of a monetary union. Today the consensus seems to have evolved favouring monetary unification, certainly in Europe.

What does this analysis teach us about the issue of whether EC countries would benefit from a monetary union? In order to answer this question we first present some data on the importance of intra-EC trade for each EC country. The data are in Table 4.1 whose most striking feature is the large difference in openness of EC countries with the rest of the Community. This leads immediately to the conclusion that the cost–benefit calculus is likely to produce very different results for the

TABLE 4.1 *Intra-Community exports of EC countries (as per cent of their GDP) in 1990*

Ireland	50.1
Belgium	49.8
Netherlands	40.0
Portugal	19.6
Germany	16.1
Denmark	13.9
France	12.5
Greece	11.6
UK	9.5
Italy	9.4
Spain	7.1

Source: EC Commission (1990).

different EC countries. For some countries with a large degree of openness relative to the other EC partners, the cost–benefit calculus is likely to tilt towards joining a European monetary union. This is most likely to be the case of the Benelux countries and Ireland. Other countries, e.g. the UK, Italy, and Spain have a relatively low openness towards the rest of the EC (in 1990). The case for joining a monetary union with the rest of Europe does not appear to be overwhelming for these countries.

The analysis implicit in Fig. 4.1 and the empirical evidence of Table 4.1 suggest that a two-speed Europe in the monetary integration process could make sense. For some countries it would be sensible from an economic point of view to tie their monetary fate to others. The most obvious case would be Benelux with Germany. Other EC countries, however, may find it advantageous to wait and see, until the 'time is ripe', i.e. until the cost–benefit calculus tilts more in favour of the benefits.

Note, however, that some countries with a low trade share may nevertheless find it advantageous to join a monetary union. Our analysis of the credibility issues makes clear that high-inflation countries, like Italy, might decide that it is in their interest to join a monetary union despite the fact that the share of trade with the members of the union is relatively low. In terms of the analysis of Fig. 4.2, this implies that the Italian authorities do not consider the loss of the exchange rate instrument costly, so that the minimum trade share that makes the union advantageous is very low. Put differently, if one is sufficiently 'monetarist', one could argue that for countries with such low degrees of openness, the benefits could still outweigh the costs, and joining a monetary union could also make sense for them from an economic point of view.

2. Monetary Union, Price and Wage Rigidities, and Labour Mobility

The cost–benefit calculus of a monetary union is also very much influenced by the degree of wage and price rigidities. As stressed in Chapter 1, countries in which the degree of wage and price rigidities is low experience lower costs when they move towards a monetary union. We show this in Fig. 4.3.

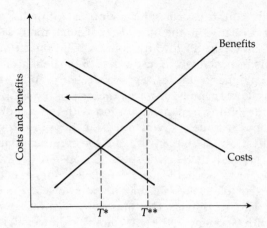

FIG. 4.3 Costs and benefits with increasing rigidities

A decline in wage and price rigidities has the effect of shifting the cost-line in Fig. 4.3 downwards. As a result, the critical point at which it becomes advantageous for a country to relinquish its national currency is lowered. More countries become candidates for a monetary union.

In a similar way, an increase in the degree of mobility of labour shifts the cost curve to the left and makes a monetary union more attractive. In this sense it can be said that, if it increases labour mobility, the single market will make a monetary union more attractive for individual EC countries. It should be noted, however, that not all forms of integration have these effects. As stressed in Chapter 2, economic integration can also lead to more regional concentration of industrial activities. This feature of the integration process changes the cost–benefit calculus, in that it shifts the cost curve to the right and makes a monetary union less attractive.

3. A Case-Study

In this section we present a case-study that vividly demonstrates the difference in the adjustment process following shocks that affect regions (or countries) differently.

During the early 1980s the industrial world was hit by a severe recession. This world-wide downturn of economic activity hit regions of the world very differently. In general, regions with an older industrial structure suffered more severely. We take two examples, Michigan in the USA, and Belgium in Europe. Both regions are of a comparable size. In Figs. 4.4 and 4.5 we present the evolution of the unemployment rate in these two regions and compare them with the total USA and European unemployment.

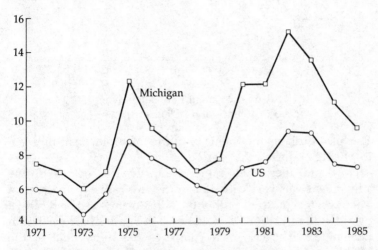

FIG. 4.4 Unemployment rate, Michigan and USA
Source: Eichengreen (1990).

We observe from these figures that unemployment increased significantly more in Michigan and Belgium than in the USA and in Europe, respectively. It should also be noted that the fact that the USA is much more integrated economically than Europe did not prevent large differentials in unemployment from emerging. In fact the differential development in unemployment rates appear to be even more pronounced in the USA than in Europe. We discussed this phenomenon in Chapter 2 where we argued that integration also leads to regional concentration. In the case of the USA, integration has also led to a large regional concentration of the automobile sector in Michigan. This sector was severely hit by the recession of the early 1980s.

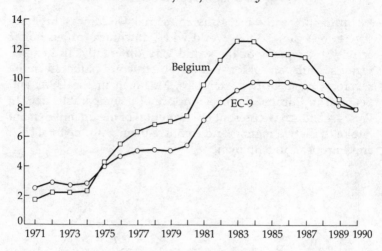

FIG. 4.5 Unemployment rate, Belgium and EC-9
Source: EC Commission (1990).

This also explains the intensity of the unemployment problem in Michigan during that period.

How did these two regions adjust? The nature of the adjustment was very different in the two cases. In the case of Michigan a significant part of the adjustment was taken care of by outward migration. This is shown in Fig. 4.6, borrowed from Eichengreen (1990), which compares the differential of the Michigan–US unemployment rate with the rate of emigration from Michigan (as a percentage of the Michigan population). Note that the percentages are not fully comparable because the denominators are different. In the case of the emigration figures, the denominator is total population, whereas in the case of the unemployment figures the denominator is the active population. The latter is typically less than half of total population. As a result, a one per cent emigration rate involves more than twice the numbers implicit in a one per cent unemployment rate. It follows that emigration from Michigan was a sizeable fraction of the unemployed, and helped to reduce the unemployment rate of that state.

In the case of Belgium the adjustment process was mainly through real exchange rate changes. In Fig. 4.7, we show the

FIG. 4.6 Michigan unemployment differential and emigration
Source: Eichengreen (1990).

differential of the Belgian–EC unemployment rate together with the real exchange rate of the Belgian franc. We observe that Belgium adjusted to the unfavourable economic developments by a real depreciation of its currency of 20–25%. This helped to restore competitiveness, and started a process of gradual recovery leading to a significant narrowing of the unemployment differential between Belgium and the EC. At the end of

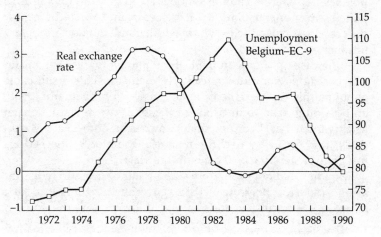

FIG. 4.7 Unemployment rate and real exchange rate, Belgium–EC
Source: EC Commission (1990).

the 1980s this differential had completely disappeared. About half of this real depreciation came about by nominal devaluations, the other half by lower cost and price developments in Belgium, compared to its main trading partners.

It should also be noted that the real depreciations of the early 1980s started to have effects on the unemployment rate in Belgium with some delay. This contrasts with the Michigan experience where the emigration reacted rather quickly to the worsening unemployment situation.

In the case of Michigan very little real depreciation took place. According to Eichengreen, regional changes in the real exchange rates in the USA were limited to a few percentage points during that period. (See Eichengreen (1990: 7). Note also that these real regional exchange rates in the USA can only change because of differential regional developments in prices.) In Belgium very little of the adjustment took the form of outward migration of Belgian unemployed workers. In 1984, for example, the number of Belgian workers who had emigrated to work elsewhere in the EC (i.e. the sum of the emigrations from all previous years) amounted to barely 40,000. This is 0.4% of the Belgian population.[2]

There is another important difference in the adjustment mechanism in these two regions. This has to do with fiscal policies. A separate chapter will be devoted to the role of fiscal policies in monetary unions. It is important to note here how differently fiscal policies work within and outside monetary unions.

In the case of Michigan the Federal budget tended to transfer purchasing power automatically to Michigan. This result came about mainly through the Federal transfers for the unemployed, and through the reduction in Federal tax revenues from Michigan. It has been estimated by Sachs and Sala-i-Martin (1989) that for every decline in state income of $1 the Federal budget transfers back 40 cents to the state.[3]

Belgium could not profit from such an intra-European redistribution. Instead, Belgium let its government budget deficit increase spectacularly and borrowed heavily in the foreign

---

[2] See T. Straubhaar (1988).

[3] Von Hagen (1991) has recently argued that this number overestimates the automatic fiscal transfers in the USA.

capital markets. This allowed it to soften the blow of the recession. It also implied that the *interregional* solidarity which was present in the USA, was substituted by an *intergenerational* solidarity within Belgium, where future generations of Belgians will have to service the government debt.

This case-study suggests that even a country like Belgium, for which the benefits of a monetary union probably outweigh the costs, would also find it costly to relinquish forever the exchange rate instrument in the face of large shocks such as the one that occurred in the early 1980s. If Belgium were to become a member of a monetary union, it would have to rely on alternative adjustment mechanisms. Since the mobility of labour between European countries is probably going to remain limited, these adjustment mechanisms are likely to be more painful than those that are initiated with exchange rate adjustments.

4. Conclusion

The arguments developed in this chapter have led to two basic conclusions. First, it is unlikely that the EC as a whole constitutes an optimal monetary union. Put differently, not all EC countries have the same interest in relinquishing their national currencies and in adhering to a European monetary union. The cost–benefit analysis of this chapter therefore also implies that a monetary unification in Europe will better suit the economic interests of the different individual countries if it can proceed with different speeds, i.e. if some countries who today feel that it is not in their national interest to do so, have the option to wait before joining the union.

Secondly, even the countries that most likely would be net gainers from a monetary union have to take into account that, faced with disturbances like the one that occurred during the early 1980s, they will pay a price for relinquishing their national currencies.

The discussion of this and the previous chapters has been based on an *economic* cost–benefit analysis. Countries may also decide to adopt a common currency for *political* reasons. A common currency may be the first step towards a political union that they wish to achieve. The economic cost–benefit analysis remains useful, however, because it gives an idea of the price some countries will have to pay to achieve these political objectives.

Part II

Monetary Integration

5

Incomplete Monetary Unions: The European Monetary System

1. Introduction

In the previous chapters we discussed the costs and benefits of full monetary unions. In the real world, there exist many monetary arrangements between nations that are far removed from full monetary union, and yet also follow rules, and constrain the national monetary policies of the participants. The best-known 'incomplete' monetary union today undoubtedly is the European Monetary System (EMS), which was instituted in 1979 among a group of EC countries. In this chapter, we analyse some of the operational problems of incomplete monetary unions, and in particular of the EMS. (See Box 5 for a discussion of some basic institutional features of the EMS.)

Pegged exchange rate systems face some important problems that have led many economists to doubt the long-run sustainability of these systems. A first problem has to do with the credibility of the fixed exchange rates. A second one concerns the way the system-wide monetary policy is determined. These problems will be the subject of the present chapter.

2. The Credibility Problem

The credibility problem of a pegged exchange rate system (like the EMS) is closely linked to the analysis of the costs and benefits of relinquishing the exchange rate instrument. It arises for two different reasons. The first reason is that the use of the exchange rate can sometimes be the least-cost instrument to

BOX 5   THE EUROPEAN MONETARY SYSTEM. SOME INSTITUTIONAL FEATURES

The European Monetary System was instituted in 1979. It came as a reaction to the large exchange rate variability of Community currencies during the 1970s, which was seen as endangering the integration process in Europe.[1]

The EMS consists of two features. the 'Exchange Rate Mechanism' (ERM) and the ECU. There is no doubt that the ERM has become the most important feature of the EMS.

Like the Bretton Woods system, the ERM can be called an 'adjustable peg' system. That is, countries participating in the ERM determine an official exchange rate (central rate) for all their currencies, and a band around these central rates within which the exchange rates can fluctuate freely. This band was set at +2.25% and −2.25% around the central rate for most member countries (Belgium, Denmark, France, Germany, Ireland, and the Netherlands). Italy was allowed to use a langer band of fluctuation (+6% and −6%) until 1990 when it decided to use the narrower band. The two newcomers in the system, Spain (1989) and the UK (1990), are allowed to use the wider band of fluctuation.

When the limits of this band (the margins) are reached the central banks of the currencies involved are committed to intervene so as to maintain the exchange rate within the band. (This intervention is called 'marginal' intervention, i.e. intervention at the margins of the band.) The commitment to intervene at the margins, however, is not absolute. Countries can (after consultation with the other members of the system) decide to change the central rates of their currency (a realignment).

These realignments were very frequent during the first half of the 1980s, when more than ten realignments took place. They have become much more infrequent since the middle of the 1980s. Since 1987 (and until the middle of 1991), no realignment has taken place.

---

[1] For a fascinating account of the discussions that led to the establishment of the EMS, see Ludlow (1982). For a more detailed description of some institutional features of the system see van Ypersele (1985).

Countries can also undertake intra-marginal interventions, i.e. they can intervene in the market when the exchange rate has not yet reached one of its margins. In order to undertake marginal interventions, the central banks need each other's currencies. For example, when the franc reaches its lower margin against the mark, the Banque de France will have to intervene by selling marks and buying franks. In order to sell marks, the Banque de France can have recourse to the 'Very Short-Term Financing Facility' (VSTFF). This is a system of credit lines between the central banks of the system. In our example, it allows the Banque de France to obtain an unlimited amount of marks which it can then sell in the foreign exchange market. In so doing, France becomes a debtor relative to Germany. It will have to repay the debt within 75 days after the end of the month in which the intervention took place.[2] Extensions of up to three months, however, are possible.

Intra-marginal interventions can be undertaken without having recourse to the VSTFF. Until 1987 it was the rule that the members of the ERM would use dollars to do intra-marginal interventions. Thus, when France wanted to limit the downward slide of the franc within the band it would buy francs and sell dollars. In 1987 the Basle–Nyborg agreement was signed among the members of the system allowing them to use the VSTFF in order to obtain a member country's currency for intra-marginal interventions.

As indicated earlier, during the first phase of the EMS, which lasted until approximately the middle of the 1980s, the realignments were frequent. Since then they have become exceptional events. The nature of the EMS, therefore, changed significantly during the 1980s. The major reason is that member countries of the system were willing to subordinate their monetary policies to the requirement of keeping fixed central rates. Some of the issues these countries encountered are analysed in the main text.

The second feature of the EMS is the existence of the ECU. The ECU is defined as a basket of currencies of the countries

---

[2] Until 1987, when the Basle–Nyborg agreement was reached, this was 45 days.

that are members of the EMS. (This is a larger group of countries than the ERM members. It includes all the EC countries.)

The value of the ECU in terms of currency i (the ECU rate of currency i) is defined as follows:

$$\text{ECU}_i = \sum_j a_j S_{ji} \tag{1}$$

where a_j is the amount of currency in the basket; S_{ji} is the price of currency j in units of currency i (the bilateral exchange rate).

In Table B5.1 we present an example of how the value of the ECU is computed in terms of French francs, using formula (1). The first column shows the a_j's. Thus, we observe that one ECU contains 1.33 French francs, 3.43 Belgian francs, 0.198 Danish kroner, 0.624 German marks etc. In the second column we have presented the exchange rates of EMS currencies in terms of the French franc. The third column is the product of the previous two columns. Each entry is the franc-equivalent of the amount of currency j in the basket. By adding up the entries in this column one obtains the price of the ECU in units of francs.

Table B5.1. The valuation of the ECU in units of French francs

Currency	a_j	S_{ji}	$a_j S_{ji}$
French franc	1.33	1	1.33
Belgian franc	3.43	0.164	0.563
Danish krone	0.198	0.880	0.174
German mark	0.624	3.388	2.114
Irish pound	0.0085	9.064	0.077
Lira	151.8	0.00456	0.692
Dutch guilder	0.2198	3.007	0.661
Pound sterling	0.0878	9.972	0.876
Greek drachma	1.44	0.0311	0.045
Spanish peseta	6.885	0.0547	0.377
Portuguese escuda	1.393	0.0383	0.053
		$\sum_j a_j S_{ji} =$	6.961

Note: The exchange rates are the market rates of the French franc in Paris on 13 June 1991.

In order to obtain the other ECU rates one can repeat the previous exercise after substituting in column 2 the exchange rates of the EMS currencies in units of the relevant currency (say currency k). Alternatively, one can use the triangular arbitrage condition, i.e.

$$ECU_k = ECU_i.S_{ik} \qquad (2)$$

where ECU_k = the price of the ECU in terms of currency k. Both procedures should yield the same result.

It should be noted that the ECU markets have evolved in such a manner that the daily ECU exchange rates are now determined by demand and supply. The ECU rates computed by equation (1) are therefore theoretical values. Arbitrage should ensure that the market rates of the ECU cannot deviate too much from its theoretical rates.

The ECU has a number of peculiar features. We analyse two of these here. First, currencies that tend to depreciate in the exchange market against the other currencies in the basket will see their share in the basket decline. This can be shown as follows. In Table B5.1 we observe that the share of the French franc in the ECU can easily be defined as the amount of francs in the basket (1.33) divided by the value of the ECU (the sum of the last column). More generally the share of currency i in the ECU is

$$b_i = a_i/ECU_i \qquad (3)$$

It can now easily be seen that as currency i depreciates against all the currencies of the basket it will also depreciate against the ECU. In other words the price of the ECU in units of currency i (ECU_i) increases. Since a_i is constant, b_i in equation (3) must decline.

This feature of the ECU by which depreciating currencies experience a decline of their weight in the basket (and appreciating currencies experience an increase of their weight) has led to problems. If the a_i's (the amount of currency i in the basket) are left unchanged, the strong EMS currencies will continuously increase in importance in the valuation of the ECU. For political reasons it was felt that this was unacceptable. As a result it was decided that every five years the a_i's are changed so as to maintain shares that are relatively stable in the long run. These changes typically implied that the amounts of the weak currencies were increased and those of the strong currencies were lowered. Many experts are convinced that this was a very unattractive feature of the ECU, since it introduced uncertainty about its future value. In the treaty of Maastricht (1991) it was agreed to solve this problem by freezing the a_i's.

A second feature of the valuation of the ECU is that when a currency depreciates (appreciates) against the other currencies in the basket, the depreciation (appreciation) against the ECU will typically be lower. This can again be seen from Table B5.1. Suppose that the French franc depreciates by 10% against all the other EMS currencies. In column 2 we now have to multiply all numbers by 1.1, except the French entry because the franc cannot depreciate against itself. Thus in the third column we still have the same entry for France. This means that the price of the ECU in terms of francs (the sum of the last column) will increase by less than 10%. The larger the share of the franc the lower its depreciation against the ECU.

What is the role of the ECU in the EMS?

The founding fathers of the EMS had high hopes about the role of the ECU in the EMS. Until today, however, the ECU has only played a limited role. In fact, it is no exaggeration to say that the exchange rate mechanism of the EMS could function exactly as it does today without the ECU.

The ECU is used as a unit of account in the EMS in the following way. Central rates are officially defined in terms of ECU rates. These central ECU rates are then translated into bilateral central rates using the triangular arbitrage condition, i.e.

$$S^*_{ij} = ECU^*_j / ECU^*_i$$

where S^*_{ij} is the central rate of currency i in units of currency j; ECU^*_i and ECU^*_j are the central ECU rates of currencies i and j respectively.

This procedure then yields the so-called parity grid (which is the matrix of bilateral central rates). It is clear that only the bilateral central rates have operational significance, because the interventions in the foreign exchange markets are carried out in national currencies and not in ECU.

The founding fathers of the EMS also wanted the ECU to be used as an instrument which would bring more symmetry into the system of interventions in the exchange markets. Therefore an indicator of divergence was defined based on the ECU. When a currency's ECU rate would diverge by more than 75% of its permitted band of fluctuation, the country in question was supposed to undertake measures to correct the divergence. This indicator of divergence was intended to work symmetrically, i.e. it would indicate which currency was on average becoming weaker or stronger against the other currencies.

This indicator of divergence never worked very well, and was quickly abandoned. The EMS did not become the symmetric system it was supposed to be. Instead relatively strong asymmetries emerged. The reasons why this happened are analysed in the main text.

adjust the economy after some disturbance. The second reason follows from the Barro–Gordon analysis stressing that governments have different reputations, which may undermine the credibility of a fixed exchange rate. Let us analyse these two problems consecutively.

2.1. *Adjustment problems lower the credibility of a fixed exchange rate*

Let us use the framework of Chapter 1 to analyse the adjustment problem. We repeat the figure of Chapter 1 (see Fig. 5.1). Suppose that the country (called France) has committed itself to keeping its exchange rate fixed. There now occurs a wage explosion in France (say like the one that happened after the 'events' of May 1968). We represent this shock by an upward movement of the supply curve of France. The effect of this shock is to lead to a current account deficit and a reduction of French output and employment. As stressed earlier in Chapter 1, if country A's wages and prices are flexible, there is nothing to worry about: French wages will decline so that the supply curve shifts downwards again. Similarly, if French workers are

Monetary Integration

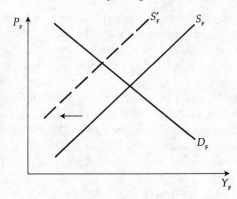

FIG. 5.1 Dilemma problem of France

willing to emigrate, the unemployment problem disappears. If, however, wages are rigid, and/or if workers are immobile, France faces a dilemma: it can reduce the current account deficit by following deflationary monetary and fiscal policies, at the cost of a still lower output and employment level; or it can increase output by expanding monetary and fiscal policies at the cost of a higher current account deficit.

With its commitment to fixed exchange rates (and given wage rigidity) there is no way France can resolve this dilemma. Note that this dilemma arises here because France pursues two objectives, while it has only one instrument, i.e. general demand policies. It has, however, one other instrument which it has chosen not to use, i.e. the exchange rate instrument. It is clear that the incentive to use this instrument in order to resolve the dilemma will be great. Speculators also will realize that the government has this incentive. As a result, they will believe it likely that a devaluation will occur in the future.

Thus, when two or more countries decide to peg their exchange rates, economic agents realize that there may be future situations in which a change in the exchange rate would minimize adjustment costs. They therefore also know that when these future situations occur, the authorities will have an incentive to renege on their commitment to keep the exchange rate fixed. As a result, such a fixed exchange rate commitment will have a low credibility, and will often be subjected to speculative crises. This credibility problem can be solved only if the authorities convince speculators that their only objective is the maintenance of the fixity of the exchange rate, whatever the output and employment costs.

2.2. *Differences in reputation lead to low credibility of a fixed exchange rate*

The Barro–Gordon model, which we discussed in Chapter 2, allows us to point to a second reason why a pegged exchange rate system suffers from a credibility problem. This analysis led to the conclusion that the high-inflation country (Italy) has a lot to gain from pegging its currency to the currency of a low-inflation country. However, Italy will find it difficult to credibly fix its exchange rate. Once the exchange rate is fixed, it has an incentive to follow inflationary policies and to devalue by surprise, so as to obtain a more favourable inflation–unemployment outcome. This, however, will be anticipated by economic agents, who will adjust their expectation of inflation. Italian inflation will be permanently higher than in Germany. This will force the authorities to devalue the currency regularly. The fixity of the exchange rate has no more credibility than announcing a low inflation rate if the Italian authorities are perceived as 'wet' and short-sighted. In addition, the regular devaluations will be anticipated, leading to large-scale speculative crises prior to the anticipated dates of realignments. The fixed exchange rate commitment will collapse.

This is a rather pessimistic view about the long-run sustainability of fixed exchange rate regimes. There are several factors, however, that tend to soften this conclusion. These factors have been important in the EMS.

3. Credibility Issues in the EMS

The surprising fact about the EMS is that, despite the existence of the credibility problems of a fixed exchange rate system, it has been in existence more than a decade. What are the factors that helped the system to overcome the credibility problem?

3.1. *Bands of fluctuation*

First, there is the existence of *bands of fluctuation*. Contrary to the Bretton Woods system, where they were relatively narrow (1% above and below the parities), in the EMS the bands have been fixed at 2.25% above and below the official parities (central rates). This allows exchange rates to move by (at most) 4.5%. For some countries (Italy until July 1990, Spain, and the UK) the bands of fluctuation have even been set at 6% below and above central rates, allowing a maximal range of fluctuation of 12%. These relatively large bands of fluctuation have been quite important in circumventing the credibility problem, in the following way.

The existence of relatively wide bands made it possible for the authorities of high-inflation countries regularly to change the exchange rate by small amounts without having to face large speculative crises prior to each expected realignment. A country with high inflation (e.g. Italy which faced a band of 12%) could devalue its currency, say, by 8% per year to offset the larger inflation rate. Given the fact that the bands of fluctuations were 12%, after each realignment the new central rate would always fall between the previously prevailing upper and lower limits. As a result, after the realignment the market exchange rate most often would not change, and could even decline. We show this feature in Fig. 5.2. We suppose that prior to the realignment date, at t_1, the exchange rate (the price of the German mark in units of lira) hits its upper limit. At t_1 the lira is devalued against the mark (the official price of the mark increases) by 8% to reflect a higher inflation of 8% in Italy as compared to Germany. One day later the previous market rate will fall between the new limits. The change that occurs on that day will usually be small. Quite often the market exchange rate will fall the day after the realignment, as speculators take their profits.

This feature of the workings of the EMS is quite different from the Bretton Woods system, where the total band of fluctuation was only 2%. We show the contrast in Fig. 5.3. Suppose again that Italy experiences a rate of inflation that is 8% higher than in the USA. At time t_1 Italy decides to devalue by 8%. The day after, the new market rate will necessarily have to jump up by at least 6%. This feature creates huge profit

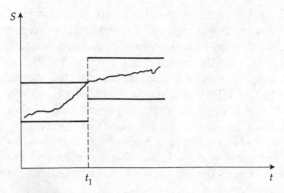

FIG. 5.2 Realignments and bands of fluctuation in the EMS

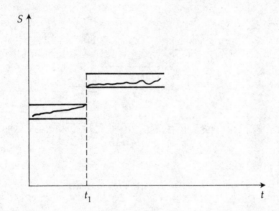

FIG. 5.3 Realignments and bands of fluctuation in the Bretton Woods system

opportunities. Speculators expecting the devaluation to occur on t_1 will be willing to bet very large amounts of money (i.e. to buy large amounts of dollars against lira) to profit from the expected gain. These speculations have a typically asymmetric feature: if the devaluation occurs on t_1 speculators make a large gain; if the devaluation does not happen they make only a small loss. The loss then arises from the fact that the interest rate on dollar assets (which have been bought) is usually smaller than the interest rate on lira assets (which have been sold). As these speculative movements are short term, this loss is very small. This one-way bet feature of speculation was very prevalent during the Bretton Woods system. It has been most often absent in the EMS, mainly because monetary authorities have been able to keep the size of the realignments small compared to the size of the band of fluctuation. We show evidence for this in Fig. 5.4 which presents the realignments of the lira and the French franc together with the bands of fluctuation. It can be seen that all the realignments of the lira were smaller than the size of the band, making it possible that after each realignment the market rate of the lira moved smoothly, without jumps. This

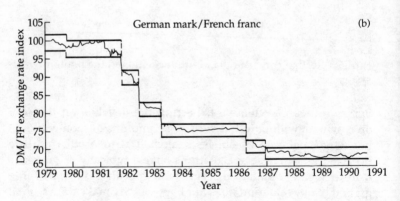

FIG. 5.4 Bilateral EMS exchange rates and band of fluctuation
Source: EC Commission (1990).

was not always the case with the French franc, however. We observe that during the period 1982–3, the three realignments of the French franc were significantly larger than the width of the band, creating large speculative gains. This period was also very turbulent. At some point, there was serious talk that the EMS would not survive the frequent speculative crises. Since that period, however, the French authorities have succeeded not only in reducing the frequency of the realignments but also in limiting the size of the realignments (relative to the size of the band). This has certainly contributed to reducing the scope for speculative gains.

We conclude from the preceding discussion that the relatively large bands of fluctuations in the EMS, while not preventing some countries from having larger rates of inflation than others, eliminated the destructive speculative movements that occur in fixed exchange rate systems with smaller bands of fluctuation. Thus, although this feature of the EMS did not solve the credibility problem of countries like Italy, it contributed towards containing its destabilizing effects in the exchange markets. An issue that arises here is what the implications will be of a move towards lower bands as foreseen by the Delors Report.

3.2. *The costs of a devaluation*

Some economists have challenged the theory that we derived from the Barro–Gordon model, i.e. that the mere fixing of the exchange rate does not allow a high-inflation country to gain credibility.[3] According to these economists, a high-inflation country announcing that it will fix its exchange rate in order to reduce inflation, faces different incentives from occasions when it announces a lowering of the rate of inflation (and lets the exchange rate float). In the Barro–Gordon model presented here, the two announcements have the same low credibility because the incentives to cheat are the same.

It can be argued, however, that the cost of a devaluation is higher than the cost of changing the announced rate of inflation. As a result, a country that has announced a fixed

---

[3] Representative economists here are Giavazzi and Pagano (1987), Giavazzi and Giovannini (1989), and Mélitz (1986).

exchange rate will have less incentive to cheat, i.e. to devalue, than a country that has announced a given rate of inflation. Rational economic agents take these differences into account, so that the fixing of the exchange rate will lead to a lower inflation rate than the alternative policy of announcing a lower rate of inflation. If this analysis is correct, one can conclude that the EMS has imposed some discipline on high-inflation countries like Italy. These countries would not have achieved the same discipline outside the EMS.

The crucial element in this reasoning has to do with the costs of a devaluation. Why are the costs of a devaluation high?

A first reason is that a change in the exchange rate has very different implications in other areas of economic life from a change in the announced rate of inflation. For example, when an EC country devalues its currency, this has implications for the Common Agricultural Policy. It generally implies that the devaluing country must increase the domestic currency prices of its agricultural products immediately,[4] or else that it introduces taxes on its agricultural exports (MCAs). These are costly changes that countries want to avoid. These problems do not exist when the country merely decides to change the announced rate of inflation.[5]

A second reason is political. The official exchange rate (the central rate) is a highly visible variable. In the context of the EMS, it cannot be changed without prior consultation with the other EMS members. The authorities of a country that devalues are often considered to have failed in their macroeconomic management. All these factors contribute to raising the perceived political costs of a devaluation. As a result, countries will quite often be reluctant to devalue their currencies, so that their incentive to cheat declines. This then increases the credibility of the fixed exchange rate arrangement.

[4] This follows from the fact that the agricultural prices are fixed each year in terms of the ECU.

[5] Of course, in that case the country must allow its exchange rate to float freely. For an EC country this has the same disturbing effects in the agricultural markets. However, as these disturbances occur continuously when an EC country allows its exchange rate to change freely, the cost of the new announcement may be perceived to be small.

3.3. The incentives of Germany

In the theoretical analysis presented so far it was assumed that Germany, to whom the high-inflation country pegs its exchange rate, is unaffected by this pegging arrangement. The question arises, however, whether the policy choices for Germany are not changed when it is drawn into a fixed exchange rate system with high-inflation countries. Is a move from a flexible exchange rate for the mark to a fixed one (with other EMS countries) not going to change the nature of German policies? Two very different answers have been given to this question.

A first answer was formulated by Rogoff (1985) and recently developed further by Fratianni and von Hagen (1990). According to these economists the movement from a flexible mark rate to a fixed one (against the other EMS currencies) changes the trade-off between inflation and unemployment in Germany. It has the effect of making the inflation–unemployment trade-off in Germany less steep. The reason is that when the German monetary authorities increase the rate of monetary expansion, the domestic inflationary effects are reduced, since part of these inflationary effects are transmitted to the other EMS countries. This change in the trade-off between inflation and unemployment in Germany has important consequences on the incentives of German policy-makers. We show the effects in Fig. 5.5.

When Germany is on a flexible exchange rate its Phillips curve is relatively steep (see the A-panel of Fig. 5.5). When Germany is in the EMS the Phillips curve is flatter. The effect of this structural change is to increase the incentives of the German authorities to introduce surprise inflation. Since economic agents are aware of this change in incentives, the equilibrium German inflation rate in the EMS will be higher than the equilibrium inflation rate when Germany allows its exchange rate to float freely. Thus, although the preferences of the German monetary authorities do not change when it becomes part of the EMS, the underlying economic structure (the short-run Phillips curve) does, thereby leading to a bigger incentive to inflate the German economy than in a floating exchange rate environment. It also follows that the gain for the high-inflation country (Italy) from tying its currency to the mark is reduced. At the same time, however, it becomes

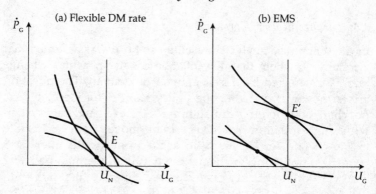

FIG. 5.5 Trade-off between inflation and unemployment in Germany

easier for Italy to join a system whose leader exhibits higher inflation.

This analysis has been challenged by, among others, Mélitz (1988). It can be argued that the movement from the flexible exchange rate regime to the EMS regime affects the trade-off between inflation and unemployment in other directions. Instead of making the short-term Phillips curve flatter, it could make it steeper. This is the case if one takes into account the fact that a surprise inflation increases domestic costs and prices. Since a country in the EMS cannot immediately devalue its currency, it makes its economy less competitive, thereby reducing the positive impact of the surprise inflation on employment. This will not be the case in a flexible exchange rate regime, where the currency will depreciate quickly, possibly even more than required for long-run equilibrium ('overshooting'). In this case the movement from a flexible exchange rate to an EMS arrangement will have the opposite effect on the equilibrium inflation rate in Germany, thereby also increasing the gain for Italy from tying its currency to the German mark.

In the preceding sections we have analysed the credibility issues arising from the fact that member countries of the EMS have different preferences about inflation and unemployment. These credibility problems make the continuing existence of the EMS in its present form uncertain. We have also seen, however, that some features of the system (in particular the relatively wide bands) have reduced its vulnerability to speculative attacks.

Another result of our analysis is that the EMS provides for potentially large gains for high-inflation countries if they can credibly fix their exchange rates with the low-inflation countries of the system. To what extent this disciplining effect of the system has been important is an empirical question. In section 7 below we present some data on inflation during the 1980s in EMS and non-EMS countries so as to find out how important this disciplining effect of the EMS has been. It will be argued that the discipline imposed by the EMS was very weak during the early phase of the workings of the system. Since the middle of the 1980s it appears to have increased. (See also Padoa-Scioppa (1988).)

4. The Liquidity Problem in Pegged Exchange Rate Systems

Every system of fixed exchange rates faces the problem of how to set the system-wide level of the money stock and interest rate. This issue essentially arises from the so-called $n-1$ problem. In a system of n countries, there are only $n-1$ exchange rates. Therefore $n-1$ monetary authorities will be forced to adjust their monetary policy instrument so as to maintain a fixed exchange rate. There will be one monetary authority which is free to set its monetary policy independently. Thus, the system has one degree of freedom. This leads to the problem of how this degree of freedom will be used. Who will be the central bank that uses this degree of freedom? Are there alternatives to the asymmetric solution where one central bank does what it likes, and others follow?

These are the questions analysed in this section. We do this by using a very simple two-country model of the money markets. Let us represent the money market of country A by the following equations:

money demand: $M_D^A = P_A L_A(Y_A, r_A)$

money supply: $M_S^A = R_A + D_A$

The money demand equation is specified in the traditional way. We assume that an increase in the price level of country A (P_A) increases the demand for money. Similarly an increase in output, Y_A, raises the demand for money. A reduction in the interest rate, r_A, increases the demand for money.

The money supply consists of two components, the international reserve component, R_A, and the domestic component of the money supply, D_A (the latter consists of bank credit to the domestic private and government sectors).

For country B we postulate similar equations, i.e.

money demand: $M_D^B = P_B L_B (Y_B, r_B)$

money supply: $M_S^B = R_B + D_B$

We will assume that there is perfect mobility of capital between these two countries. This allows us to use the interest-parity condition, which we specify as follows:

$r_A = r_B + \mu$

where μ is the expected rate of depreciation of the currency of country A.

This relationship is also called the 'open interest parity'. It says that if economic agents expect a depreciation of currency A, the interest rate of country A will have to exceed the interest rate of country B in order to compensate holders of assets of country A for the expected loss.

Now suppose countries A and B decide to fix their exchange rate. Let us also assume that economic agents do not expect that the exchange rate will be adjusted in the future. This means that $\mu = 0$. The interest rates in the two countries will be identical.

We can now represent the equilibrium of this system graphically as follows (see Fig. 5.6). The downward-sloping curve is the money demand curve. The money supply is represented by the vertical lines M_1^A and M_1^B. Money market equilibrium in both countries is obtained where demand and supply intersect (points E and F). In addition, given the interest-parity condition, the interest rates must be equal.

It is clear from Fig. 5.6 that there are many combinations of such points that bring about equilibrium in this system. Consider, for example, the points G and H. At these two points

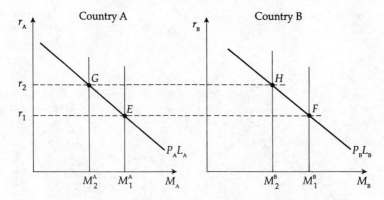

FIG. 5.6 The $n-1$ problem in a two-country monetary model

demand and supply of money in the two countries are equal, and the interest rates are also equalized. It is easy to see that there are infinitely many combinations that will satisfy these equilibrium conditions. Each of these combinations will produce one level of the interest rate and one of the money stock. One can say that the fixed exchange rate arrangement is compatible with any possible *level* of the interest rates and of the money stocks. There is a fundamental indeterminacy in this system. This follows from the $n-1$ problem, which, as we have seen, produces one degree of freedom in the system.

How can this indeterminacy be solved? We discuss two possible solutions, one is asymmetric (hegemonic), the other is symmetric (co-operative).

4.1. The asymmetric (hegemonic) solution

The first solution to the problem consists in allowing one country to take a leadership role. Suppose, for example, that country A is the leader and that it fixes its money stock independently, say at the level M_1^A (see Fig. 5.7). This then fixes the interest rate in country A at the level r_1. Country B now has no choice any more. Its interest rate will have to be the same as in country A. Given the money demand in country B, this then uniquely determines the money supply in country B (M_1^B) that will be needed to have equilibrium. Country B has to accept

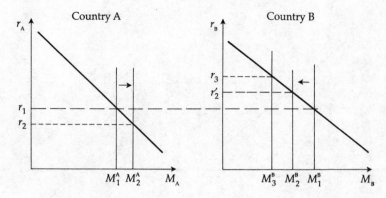

FIG. 5.7 Symmetric and asymmetric adjustment to a speculative movement

this money supply. It cannot follow an independent monetary policy.

In this asymmetric arrangement, country A takes on the role of anchoring the money stock in the system. The degree of freedom in the system is used by country A to set its monetary policy independently.

4.2. *The symmetric (co-operative) solution*

A second possibility is for the two countries to decide jointly about the level of their money stocks and interest rates. Thus, this solution requires co-operation. For example, in Fig. 5.7, the two countries could decide jointly that the money stocks in the two countries will be equal to M_1^A and M_1^B.

The original blueprint of the EMS was aimed at promoting this co-operative solution. In particular, the use of the ECU as an indicator of divergence was seen as an instrument that would promote symmetry in the system. As explained in Box 5, when the market exchange rates of a currency deviated too much from its central rates, this would show in the indicator of divergence. The country involved would then be singled out to take necessary action. This implied that a country with a strong (weak) currency would be required to expand (contract) its monetary policies.

A second way the symmetric solution was intended to work was through the system of interventions in the foreign exchange markets. The rule was that when two currencies hit their upper limits, the intervention would be in each other's currency, so that the monetary effect in the two countries would be symmetrical.

We illustrate this symmetric intervention system in Fig. 5.7. We assume that doubts have arisen about the fixity of the exchange rate of currency A against currency B, and that economic agents expect a *future* devaluation of currency B. According to the interest-parity condition, this requires an increase in the interest rate of country B relative to the interest rate of country A. In the foreign exchange market the following will happen. The expectation of a future devaluation of currency B leads speculators to sell currency B against currency A. In order to prevent the market rate of currency B from dropping below its limit against A, the central bank of country B must buy its own currency and sell currency A. (The latter it will typically obtain through the system of short-term financing, which forces country A to provide the necessary amounts of its currency to country B.) The result of this intervention on the money stocks is symmetric: country B's money stock declines, and country A's money stock increases. The latter arises from the fact that the sale of currency A by country B increases the amount of currency A in circulation. We represent this symmetric effect in Fig. 5.7 by a leftward shift of the money stock line in country B (from M_1^B to M_2^B) and a rightward shift of the money stock line in country A (from M_1^A to M_2^A). As a result, the interest rate in country B increases to r'_2, whereas it declines in country A to r_2. Thus, the speculative disturbance is taken care of by a symmetric adjustment, in which country A allows its money stock to increase and its interest rate to decline, and country B allows the opposite to occur.

As a matter of fact, the symmetric solution, as we just described it, has generally not worked well. In particular, when a speculative crisis arose, requiring intervention in the foreign exchange market, the strong-currency country (Germany) has generally been unwilling to allow its money stock to increase and its interest rate to decline. This Germany has achieved by using *sterilization policies*, i.e. by offsetting the expansionary effects of the interventions in the foreign exchange market by reverse operations of the Bundesbank. Thus, when the central bank of the weak-currency country sold marks (against its own currency) the Bundesbank has usually bought these marks back through open market operations. The effect of these sterilization policies then was that the German money stock was not (or only slightly) affected by the foreign exchange market operations of the weak-currency countries.

The implication of this asymmetry is that the weak currency is forced to do all the monetary adjustment. In Fig. 5.7 we see that country B is now forced to reduce its money stock to the level given by M_3^B, and to allow the interest rate to increase to r_3. The money stock of country A remains unchanged at M_1^A in this asymmetric adjustment system.

Despite the original intentions of the founding fathers of the EMS, the system has evolved into an asymmetric one. (See Box 6, however, where empirical literature is discussed indicating that, although the EMS is asymmetric, there is more monetary interdependence than meets the eye.) Such asymmetric arrangements are very common in fixed exchange rate systems. In the Bretton Woods system, the USA took on this role. In the EMS, Germany has taken the anchoring role.

Several issues arise here. First, the question is why a particular country is selected as a leader, and not another one. Why did Germany become the leader in the EMS? This question will be analysed in section 6 below. Secondly, what are the characteristics of these asymmetric (sometimes also called hegemonic) arrangements as compared to symmetric systems, where countries decide jointly about the system-wide money stock and interest rate, or where they allow rules to lead to symmetric adjustments?

5. Symmetric and Asymmetric Systems Compared

An asymmetric system has a number of important advantages, together with disadvantages. Let us analyse the advantages first. One important advantage of this system is that it imposes a lot of discipline on the peripheral country. Suppose the latter should decide to increase its money stock. This would

BOX 6   IS THE EMS A DM ZONE?

There is now a general consensus that Germany has played a dominant role in the EMS. In the previous section we examined the reasons for this. This has led many observers to interpret the EMS as a mark zone, in which the German authorities independently set their monetary policies, and the other EMS members passively adjust to these policy actions of the German authorities.

There is now a substantial amount of empirical evidence indicating that this interpretation of the workings of the EMS is too extreme. Econometric analysis of the movements of interest rates and monetary aggregates within the EMS reveals that although Germany is the dominant player, other countries have maintained some degree of limited control over their interest rates and money stocks (during relatively short periods of time). This limited autonomy was made possible, in the case of France and Italy, by the existence of capital controls that only in 1990 were completely abolished. (For evidence, see De Grauwe (1989), Fratianni and von Hagen (1990), Weber (1990), and Kool and Koedijk (1991).) With the abolition of capital controls this relative autonomy is likely to be impaired.

The econometric evidence also shows that the causal relation between German interest rates and monetary aggregates on the one hand and the interest rates and monetary aggregates in the rest of the system on the other is not one-way. There is some (albeit weaker) influence from other EMS countries on Germany. This suggests that the German authorities have been responsive to what happened in the rest of the system (see Fratianni and von Hagen (1990)). This also indicates that the nature of the monetary interdependencies within the system is more complex than the simple mark-zone view of the EMS suggests.

immediately lead to a drain on the international reserves of the central bank of the peripheral country, because residents would seek a riskless higher rate of return in the centre country. The peripheral country would be forced almost instantaneously to lower its money stock again.

It should be noted here that in the asymmetric arrangement the flow of liquidity from the periphery to the centre country does not affect the money stock in the latter country. In this asymmetric system, the centre country automatically sterilizes the liquidity inflow by reverse open market operations. If it did not do so, the monetary expansion engineered by the peripheral country would lead to an increase of the money stock in the centre country. That country would then also lose its function of an anchor for the whole system.

There are other features of the asymmetric system, however, that make it less attractive. These have to do with the way unsynchronized business cycles affect the money markets. In order to show this, we suppose that the peripheral country experiences a recession. We represent this effect in the money markets of the two countries in Fig. 5.8. The recession in the peripheral country shifts the demand for money downwards as shown in Fig. 5.8. This has the effect of reducing the interest rate in that country. However, interest parity (and assuming that no future devaluations are expected) makes it impossible for the interest rate to decline below the centre country's interest rate. Since in the centre country no change in the money demand occurs, and its authorities continue to fix the domestic money supply, the interest rate in the centre country cannot change. The result is that the money supply in the peripheral country must automatically decline. This comes about as follows. The downward pressure on the peripheral country's interest rate leads to an outflow of capital to the centre country. This reduces the money stock in the peripheral country, and would increase the money stock in the centre country. However, as the authorities of that country are committed to fix their supply of money, they automatically sterilize the reserve inflow by open market sales of securities.

The less attractive feature of this adjustment mechanism is that a recession which originates in the peripheral country is made worse by a contraction of the country's money stock. The

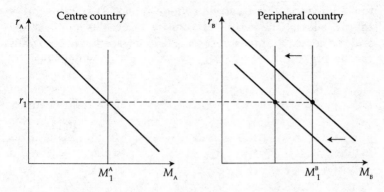

FIG. 5.8 The effects of a recession at the periphery

opposite occurs when a boom originates in the peripheral country. In that case the boom is automatically accommodated by an increase in the money stock of the peripheral country, because the upward pressure on its interest rate leads to a capital inflow. (The reader can work out this case for herself/ himself using the model of Fig. 5.8.) The result is that the business cycles in the peripheral country are likely to be made more intense by the procyclical movements of the money stock of the periphery.

It is clear that this asymmetric system of monetary control is not very efficient at dealing with asymmetric shocks such as unsynchronized business cycles. The problem is that while the centre country tries to stabilize its money stock without regard to what happens in the rest of the system, it helps to make the money stock volatile in the peripheral country. In this system, there is no one responsible for the money stock of the whole system.

The previous analysis also makes clear that the asymmetric system in which the centre country rigidly fixes its money supply does not guarantee that the money stock will be stable in the system as a whole when asymmetric shocks occur. The symmetric system of monetary control would be more successful in stabilizing the system's money stock when unsynchronized business cycles occur. In order to show this, we take the case of a recession in the peripheral country again. We now assume that the central banks of the centre and the periphery co-operate to stabilize the whole system's money stock. They can achieve this as follows. The peripheral country reduces its money stock, and the centre country increases its money stock. We show this case in Fig. 5.9.

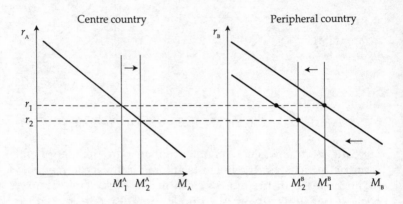

F IG . 5.9 A recession at the periphery in a symmetric system

The effect of this co-ordinated approach is that the total money supply is kept unchanged. Note that this result will come about automatically if the centre country does not sterilize the inflows of reserves that are triggered by the decline in the interest rate of the peripheral country.

The problems of monetary control that arise in an asymmetric system when asymmetric shocks occur are likely to lead to conflicts about the kind of monetary policy to be followed for the whole system. For example, during a recession originating in the peripheral countries, these will find that the monetary policies they have to endure are inappropriate. Pressures on the centre country will certainly be exerted. These conflicts of interests will have to be dealt with in one way or another.

The preceding discussion also suggests that an asymmetric system may not survive in the long run. Too much conflict will exist about the appropriate monetary policies for the system as a whole. Peripheral countries, especially if they are similar in size to the centre country (as is the case in the present EMS), may not be willing to subject their national interests to the survival of the system. In the end, more explicit co-operative arrangements may be necessary.

6. The Choice of a Leader in the EMS

In the previous sections it was argued that asymmetric arrangements are often used to 'anchor' the money stock in a fixed exchange rate system. In this section we analyse the question of why fixed exchange rate systems tend to end up with one leader and many followers. In addition, we determine the factors that decide who becomes the leader. In order to do so, we return to the Barro–Gordon model of two countries. Let us call these two countries Germany and Italy again.

We take as a starting point Fig. 2.12 (Chapter 2). Suppose, as before, that Germany and Italy have decided to fix their exchange rate. In principle, this arrangement can work with any level of the common inflation rate. This could be the German inflation rate. It could also be the Italian inflation rate, or any other inflation rate, as long as it is the same one for both countries. This requirement follows from the purchasing power parity condition which we have imposed.

Which inflation rate will be most beneficial for the two countries? It can easily be shown that this is the lower (German) inflation rate. In order to see this, suppose first that Italy decides to accept the German inflation rate, and suppose that the fixing of the exchange rate can be made credible. Then the welfare gain for Italy will be given by the movement of the inflation rate from E to F (see Fig. 5.10). Italy has now a lower inflation rate at no cost in terms of unemployment.[6]

Consider now the alternative. Suppose Germany accepted the Italian inflation rate. The inflation equilibrium would now be given by point G. This is a clear loss of welfare in Germany, without any gain in Italy. There is no reason to assume that Germany would be willing to strike a deal which would make it worse off, and which would not make Italy any better off. In fact, it can also be seen that Germany has no incentive at all to accept any other inflation rate than the one it had prior to the

---

[6] We abstract from the possible short-run losses when Italy disinflates and unemployment increases temporarily. See sect. 7.

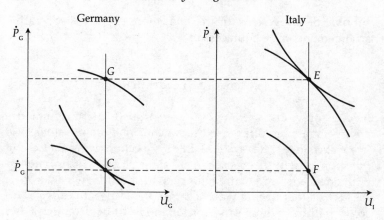

F I G. 5.10 The selection of a leader in the EMS

establishment of the fixed exchange rate. Conversely, Italy has an incentive to aim for the lower German inflation rate. Under those conditions, it is quite easy to understand that Italy will be glad to accept the leadership of Germany in determining the system-wide inflation rate. This is an arrangement that maximizes welfare in Italy without reducing welfare in Germany.

The previous analysis stresses that the leadership position of a country depends on its reputation in maintaining a low inflation equilibrium. Reputations can change, however. For example, political and institutional changes may affect the preferences of the centre country's authorities, leading to a higher inflation equilibrium. Similarly, an increase in the natural unemployment rate may bring about a higher inflation equilibrium. These changes are likely to jeopardize the leadership position of the centre country, as other countries may decide to stop pegging their exchange rates to that country, and to look for another low-inflation country to take up the role of the leader.

Such changes in leadership positions are likely to lead to great disturbances. They can also endanger the stability of the system, and may lead to its downfall. This is what happened in the Bretton Woods system when the USA stopped being the low-inflation country of the system. Other countries lost their incentives to peg their currencies to the dollar. One should not exclude the possibility that such disturbances occur in the EMS.

7. Disinflation in the EMS during the 1980s

The disinflation in the EMS since the early 1980s has been substantial. From a peak of 11% in 1980, the rate of inflation within the system declined to an average of 2% in 1988. This decline in the inflation rate within the EMS, however, is not exceptional when we compare it with the disinflation that has occurred in the rest of the industrialized world during the same period. This is made clear from Fig. 5.11 which shows the average inflation rates in the EMS and in the rest of the OECD countries. From this figure we learn that the disinflation process in the EMS was initially slower than in the rest of the OECD area. Since 1986, however, the EMS countries have caught up

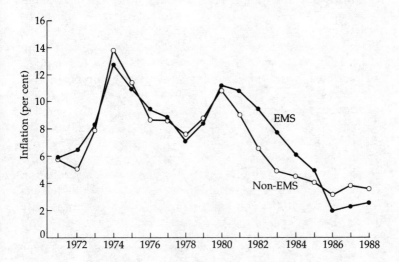

FIG. 5.11 Inflation (CPI) in EMS and non-EMS (OECD)
Note: The EMS and non-EMS inflation rates are weighted averages of national inflation rates using GDP as weights.
Source: OECD (1990).

and have maintained a lower inflation rate than in these other countries.

The low inflation rates achieved within the EMS since 1986 have led to a widespread belief that there is a disciplining feature in the EMS arrangement that facilitates disinflation. This view was discussed in previous sections, and has been given a more formal content by Giavazzi and Pagano (1988), Giavazzi and Giovannini (1989), and Mélitz (1988).[7]

Policies of disinflation usually lead to temporary increases in unemployment. This was also the case in the 1980s. In Fig. 5.12 we present the unemployment trends in the EMS and in the non-EMS countries. The most striking feature of this figure is the fact that since 1984 the unemployment experience of the two groups of countries has been dramatically different. Whereas in the non-EMS OECD countries, unemployment started declining substantially from 1983, it continued to increase in the EMS. Since 1984, EMS unemployment has stabilized around 10%.

The very different experiences of EMS and non-EMS OECD countries are also made vivid in Figs. 5.13 and 5.14 which

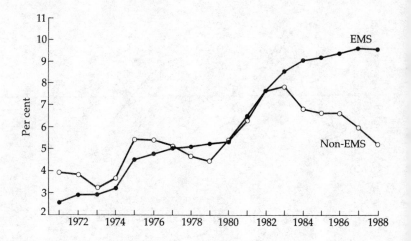

FIG. 5.12 Unemployment in EMS and non-EMS (OECD)
Source: OECD (1990).

[7] For sceptical notes see Fratianni (1988), Fratianni and von Hagen (1990), Dornbusch (1989), and Collins (1988).

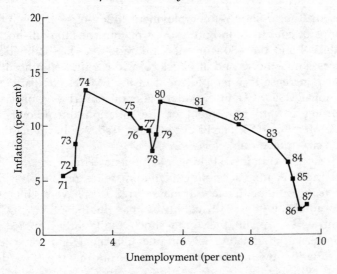

FIG. 5.13 Inflation–Unemployment (EMS)
Source: Computed from OECD (1990).

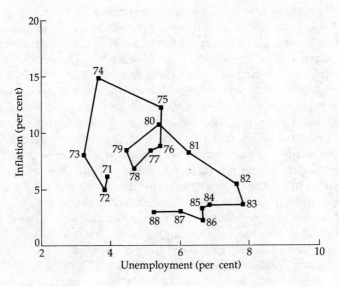

FIG. 5.14 Inflation–Unemployment non-EMS (OECD)
Source: Computed from OECD (1990).

present the inflation–unemployment trade-offs in the two groups of countries. In both groups of countries the oil shocks of 1973–4 and 1979–80 worsened the trade-off. The disinflation process since the second oil shock coincides with a significantly higher increase in unemployment in the EMS as compared to the non-EMS OECD. In the latter group of countries we observe a strong inward movement of the inflation–unemployment trade-off since 1983. The EMS countries' trade-off has remained at a very unfavourable level since 1984.

These are certainly striking phenomena. How can they be explained? A first possible explanation relies on supply-side effects. It could be that labour market rigidities have been more pronounced in the EMS countries than in the other OECD countries. As a result, the supply shocks of the early 1980s led to an increase in the natural level of unemployment, and prevented the inflation–unemployment trade-offs from moving inwards. Some evidence in support of this hypothesis is given in De Grauwe (1990).

This explanation, however, is not sufficient. It also appears that, at least initially, the EMS provided little of the disciplining effects that we discussed in previous sections.[8] The reason was that there was little credibility in the fixity of the exchange rates. Countries like France and Italy devalued regularly during the first half of the 1980s, and therefore imported little inflationary discipline from Germany. A change occurred around the middle of the 1980s. France and (to a lesser degree) Italy made it clear that they were committed to maintaining more rigid exchange rates with the low-inflation country in the system. This is also the time that the inflation record of these countries improved. However, we also observe that the unemployment rate remained stubbornly high. These changes certainly helped to improve the credibility of the fixed exchange rates within the system. They demonstrated to economic agents that the monetary authorities of these countries were giving an overriding priority to keeping inflation low, even if this contributed to more (temporary) unemployment.

One can conclude that the disciplining effects in the EMS were weak during the first half of the 1980s. During the second

---

[8] For evidence see Fratianni and von Hagen (1990) and Weber (1990).

half of the 1980s, however, there is evidence that the inflation-discipline imposed by the system started to work and that the fixity of the exchange rates gained credibility. It is thus not clear whether the EMS reduced the cost of disinflation, compared to other monetary arrangements.

8. Conclusion

In this chapter we have analysed the workings of the European Monetary System. Contrary to the predictions of many economists, the EMS has survived now for more than a decade. In this chapter we have argued that the EMS has been able to cope with two problems of fixed exchange rate systems, i.e. the credibility and the liquidity problems, which in the past have often led to the collapse of fixed exchange rate adjustments. We also argued, however, that in the present EMS there are problems that make the continuing survival of the system, in its present form, uncertain. This uncertainty makes it necessary to strengthen the system so that it can evolve towards a full monetary union.

BOX 7   ZONE MODELS AND THE EUROPEAN MONETARY SYSTEM

The exchange rate mechanism of the EMS operates with a band within which the exchange rate can move freely. Once the edges of the band are reached, however, the monetary authorities are committed to intervene so as to prevent the exchange rate from moving outside the band. This feature of the system has led theorists to speculate about the behaviour of the exchange rate in such a system. This has led to the so-called target-zone models pioneered by Krugman (1989) and developed further by (among others) Svensson (1990) and Bertola and Svensson (1990).

The basic idea of these models is strikingly simple (although the mathematics is not). Suppose speculators are fully confident that the exchange rate will not go beyond the limits of the band because they are convinced that the monetary authorities will successfully defend these limits. Assume in addition that there are stochastic disturbances in the fundamental variables that determine the exchange rate. (These fundamentals could be the money stock, the price level, etc.). How is the relationship between these fundamentals and the exchange rate going to look? The answer is given in Fig. B7.1. On the vertical axis we show the exchange rate (S_t), on the horizontal axis the fundamental variable (f_t). The two horizontal lines (S_U and S_L represent the limits between which the exchange rate will fluctuate. The fluctuations of the fundamental variable around f^* lead to fluctuations of the exchange rate. In a world of rational expectations, the exchange rate must lie on the S-shaped curve. That is, as the exchange rate comes closer to, say, the upper limit of the band, speculators know that the authorities' commitment will prevent the exchange rate from moving beyond the limit. Therefore, the probability that the exchange rate increases in the future declines as we move closer to the limit, and the probability of a decline increases. Speculators will find it advantageous to sell foreign exchange, thereby preventing the exchange rate from actually reaching the limit. Speculation will be stabilizing, and the authorities will not

have to intervene. This result only holds if the credibility of the band is very strong. If this is not the case, speculation will not be stabilizing. Speculators then will test the resolve of the authorities, forcing them to intervene in the market.

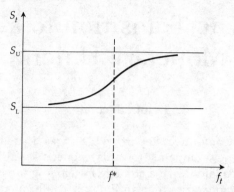

FIG. B7.1 Exchange rate and the fundamental variable in a target-zone model

6

The Transition to a Monetary Union

1. Introduction

The Delors Committee Report, which was issued in 1989, provided a new impetus towards monetary unification in Europe. It also laid down a strategy for moving forward in the direction of monetary union in Europe. The basic philosophy behind this strategy is one of gradualism, i.e. the process of monetary unification is to proceed in stages. At each stage the degree of convergence and of co-operation is increased, so that in the final stage a full monetary union can be introduced. At the Maastricht Summit Meeting of 1991 the heads of states formally agreed to follow this strategy towards monetary union in Europe.

In this chapter we first discuss the integration strategy of the Maastricht Treaty. We then study the question of alternative integration strategies. More specifically we contrast the gradual approach to the shock therapy. Finally, we ask the question of the usefulness of alternative approaches based on a parallel currency.

2. The Maastricht Treaty: A Three-Stage Approach

The Delors Report contains a blueprint for moving towards monetary union in three stages.[1] At the summit meeting of Maastricht, the heads of state of the Community signed a treaty which formalized this approach.

In the first stage (which began on 1 July 1990), the EMS

[1] See Delors Report (1989).

countries abolished all remaining capital controls.[2] The degree of monetary co-operation among the EMS central banks was strengthened, and negotiations were started that, in December 1991, led to the Maastricht Treaty. This Treaty contains a formal agreement to establish a European Central Bank (ECB) at the latest in 1999, and it defines the next stages towards monetary union. During the first stage, which lasts until 31 December 1993, realignments remain possible.

The second stage will start on 1 January 1994. A new institution, the European Monetary Institute (EMI), will then be created. It will operate only during this second stage, and is in a sense the precursor of the European Central Bank. Its functions will be limited, and will be geared mainly towards strengthening monetary co-operation between national central banks.

At the start of the third and final stage the exchange rates between the national currencies will be irrevocably fixed. In addition, the European Central Bank will start its operations. The ECB will issue the European currency, which will become a currency in its own right. The transition to this final stage of monetary union, however, is made conditional on a number of 'convergence criteria'. A country can only join the union if:

(1) its inflation rate is not more than 1.5% higher than the average of the three lowest inflation rates in the EMS;

(2) its long-term interest rate is not more than 2% higher than the average observed in the three low inflation countries;

(3) it has not experienced a devaluation during two years preceding the entrance in the union;

(4) its government budget deficit is not higher than 3% of its GDP;

(5) its government debt is not higher than 60% of its GDP.

If a majority of EMS countries satisfy these conditions, the third stage could already start at the end of 1996. If this is not the case, the third stage has to start at the latest on 1 January 1999, with those countries that satisfy the criteria. The UK has maintained the right to opt out, and Denmark to subject the agreement to a national referendum.

The Maastricht Treaty embodies two principles. One is that

[2] This step was important only for France and Italy which still had capital controls before that date.

BOX 8   THE GERMAN MONETARY UNIFICATION OF 1990

On 1 July 1990, West and East Germany instituted monetary union. This decision can certainly be called a shock-therapy approach towards monetary union. On that day the East-German mark was taken out of circulation, and was replaced by the West German mark (DM).

Technically, this operation was a great success. The DM became legal tender immediately in the whole of Germany. The West German banking system was quite successful in creating a payments system in the East which was based on the DM. The experiment clearly demonstrates that, from a technical point of view, a shock therapy can work.

The economic effects of this German shock therapy, however, do not seem to have been as successful, at least in the immediate aftermath of the introduction of the DM in East Germany. One year after the monetary union in Germany, output in the Eastern part of the country dropped to 50% of the level it had reached prior to the union. Unemployment increased dramatically. This seems to suggest that the shock therapy which was applied in East Germany was too quick and too harsh.[3]

Does this mean that the case for a shock therapy for a European monetary union is weakened? Not necessarily. It is important to realize that the German monetary unification was quite a special and unique experiment. First, the German monetary unification coincided with a complete overhaul of the East German planning system. The introduction of the DM in East Germany went together with an immediate opening up of the East German economy that up to that time had been closed to external competition. This led to an almost instantaneous collapse of large parts of East German industry which was unable to compete with Western firms.

A quick monetary union between the EC countries would be of a totally different nature. The EC countries have broadly

[3] This did not come as a total surprise to most economists, e.g. the Sachverständigenrat (1990) warned the German government in Jan. 1990 not to move too fast towards monetary union between East and West Germany.

similar economic systems. In addition, they opened up their markets long ago. Introducing a European currency in these countries would not have these destructive effects that we have observed in East Germany.

Secondly, the choice of the rate at which the old mark was converted into DM was very problematic. Prior to unification, one East German mark traded at a rate of 6 marks = 1 DM in the black market. Despite this low market rate of the East German mark, the German authorities decided to use a rate of 1 mark = 1 DM for the conversion of East German wages. This turned out to be an extremely overvalued exchange rate. It also implied that the East German worker's wage, converted into DM, was much too high (given the productivity of East German workers) to be competitive in comparison with the West German wage level. This unrealistically high conversion rate also contributed towards the collapse of East German industry immediately after unification.

The choice of a correct conversion rate when a new currency is introduced in Europe is of great importance. A wrong choice could force countries into an unfavourable competitive situation. In the context of European monetary unification, it is unlikely, however, that the same large error would be made in selecting the right conversion rate as in the case of East Germany, where much uncertainty existed concerning the correct exchange rate to apply.

Finally it is important to stress here that the German monetary unification also led to large fiscal transfers from West to East Germany. These transfers allowed East German households actually to increase their real disposable income, despite the massive decline in output. It is obvious that without these fiscal transfers German monetary union would have been strained to the extreme, as it would have led to a sudden pauperization of East Germany.

In a sense it can be said that today the two Germanies form an optimum currency area. The centralization of the fiscal system which is now a fact, allows the large asymmetric shocks to which East Germany was subjected, to be compensated by transfers from the Western part of the country. Thus, German monetary unification illustrates the importance of the political will to form a union. Prior to 1990, East and West

Germany were economically so different that a monetary union seemed inconceivable. However, the strong political will to unify the country created the economic conditions (including a unified fiscal system) to make a currency union possible in Germany.

the transition to monetary union should be gradual. The other is that not all EC countries have to join a monetary union at the same time.

From the wording of the Treaty, it is not clear whether at the start of the third stage, the national currencies will be replaced by the ECU, or whether they will continue to circulate alongside the ECU. The issues that arise because of this ambiguity are discussed in the next chapter.

3. Gradualism Versus Shock Therapy in Monetary Unification

The Delors Report and the Maastricht Treaty have opted for gradualism in the process towards monetary union.

There is, however, an alternative which would consist in immediately introducing a full monetary union in Europe. The recent monetary unification of East and West Germany certainly proves that such a strategy can work (see Box 8 on the German monetary unification of 1990). In fact most of the monetary unions in history have been of the shock-therapy type. There are very few successful processes of monetary unification that proceeded gradually.[4]

Let us contrast these two strategies, and discuss their advantages and disadvantages. We again use the Barro–Gordon model for open economies to analyse the main issues. Suppose, as before, that there are two countries, Germany and Italy. Both decide to form a full monetary union. This is understood to be a situation in which one common currency circulates in both countries, and in which one central bank has the sole authority to issue that currency.[5] Let us first see how shock therapy could be implemented.

[4] For a history of the German and Italian monetary unifications see Holtfrerich (1989) and Sannucci (1989).

[5] The Delors Report allows for two possible monetary unions. There is one in which the national currencies would continue to circulate, however, with

Fig. 6.1 presents the diagram that we used in the previous chapter. Suppose that Germany and Italy agree that the Bundesbank becomes the central bank of the two countries and that the mark becomes the money to be used as legal tender in the two countries. To take care of political sensitivities these two countries could agree to give a new name to the Bundesbank, to call it the Eurofed, and to rename the mark as an ECU.[6]

This decision can be implemented on a particular day, say E-day: German and Italian citizens are told to convert their marks and their lire into ECUs at a given conversion rate. One could use here the central rates of these currencies against the ECU. For example, if on the day prior to E-day the ECU rate of the lira is 1,555, Italian citizens present 1,555 lire on E-day to obtain one ECU. A similar conversion takes place in Germany. Thus, this shock therapy amounts to a monetary reform.

It can now easily be seen that there is a great advantage for Italy to proceed in this way. We show this in Fig. 6.1. Prior to E-day, the inflation equilibrium in Italy was given by point E.

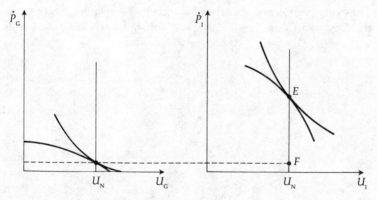

FIG. 6.1 Advantages of a shock therapy

'irrevocably' fixed exchange rates; there is another in which a common currency would circulate, and the national currencies would disappear. We return to these two views of the final stage of the monetary union in sect. 2 of Ch. 7, where we argue that only the second view is likely to be credible.

[6] This renaming trick may seem innocuous. There are, however, more substantive political problems underlying this change of name. Here we disregard these problems. We return to them in the next chapter.

After E-day, Italy can immediately move to point *F*, the German (European) inflation rate without any cost in terms of unemployment. The ECU (a money issued by the Bundesbank, which we gave a new name) is now circulating in Italy, and will be subject to the German inflation rate. Economic agents realize this, and are willing instantaneously to reduce their expectation about the inflation rate that will prevail in Italy. Thus, Italy can immediately profit from the reputation of the German central bank. By taking over the money and the institutions of the low-inflation country, Italy can instantaneously capture a large welfare gain from the monetary union. We conclude that there is a great advantage from a shock therapy (a monetary reform).

We can now contrast the shock therapy (monetary reform) with the gradual strategy. Suppose that Germany and Italy agree to move towards a monetary union slowly. That is, they agree that before the crucial step towards full monetary union is taken, the Italian inflation rate should converge towards the low German inflation rate. As a result, the Italian authorities announce a policy of gradual reduction of the inflation rate. They also announce that they will keep the exchange rate with the German mark fixed. However, future devaluations are not excluded.

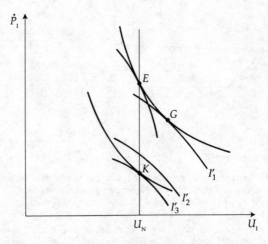

FIG. 6.2 The cost of gradual disinflation in Italy

In order to analyse the problem Italy is going to face, we use the Barro–Gordon model as extended by Backus and Driffill (1985), which we represent in Fig. 6.2. Prior to the announcement of the policy of gradual convergence, equilibrium was located at point *E*. The announcement of the new policy can be interpreted as a change in priorities by the Italian authorities. They are now willing to accept more (temporary) unemployment in order to reduce inflation. We represent this change in policy preferences by the indifference curves I'_1, I'_2, which are flatter than the initial ones. The problem, however, is that economic agents are uncertain about the seriousness of this 'conversion'. As a result, they will not be willing to believe this announcement. They will want proof. This can be obtained only from observed facts. Economic agents will be willing to believe the seriousness of the authorities only after they have observed that the authorities have implemented disinflation policies and that they are willing to let unemployment increase. As a result, it will be necessary for the economy to move to point *G*. At that point, the Italian authorities reveal their changed preferences, i.e. the slope of the short-term Phillips curve is equal to the new indifference curve. Thus economic agents observe from the facts that these preferences have changed and that the authorities are now willing to let unemployment increase more in order to achieve a given reduction of inflation.

This situation will gradually lead to a change in expectations, allowing the short-term Phillips curve to shift downwards. We move to point *K*. It follows that this transition process will be a slow and costly one. It should be noted that this is the strategy that countries like Italy and France have applied from the second half of the 1980s on. As was demonstrated in the previous chapter, this disinflation process was slow and painful.

Some economists have argued that this strategy of slow convergence of the inflation rate in the high-inflation countries to the German level is risky, and in the end may fail to bring the inflation rates to equality. The reason for drawing this pessimistic conclusion can be explained as follows. It is unlikely that the new Italian policies will convince economic agents that the Italian authorities are as 'hard-nosed' about inflation as the

German authorities. Therefore, the new inflation equilibrium (at *K*) will still be higher than in Germany (see Fig. 6.2). Thus, the Italian inflation rate will not converge to the German one, but will hover above it.

This situation leads immediately to a credibility problem. As the Italian inflation rate remains above the German one, the price *levels* of the two countries will tend to diverge continuously. This leads to a continuous loss of competitiveness of Italian industry. In the end this situation becomes unsustainable, and there will be no option but a devaluation. Convergence will be all the more difficult thereafter.

There is now a lot of evidence that this is the problem the Italian economy has faced since the middle of the 1980s. We show some evidence in Figs. 6.3 to 6.5. In Fig. 6.3, we observe that since 1983–84 the inflation rate in Italy has approached the German one without, however, moving towards equality with it.

During the 1980s the lira was devalued by less than the inflation differential with Germany, and since 1987 the lira has

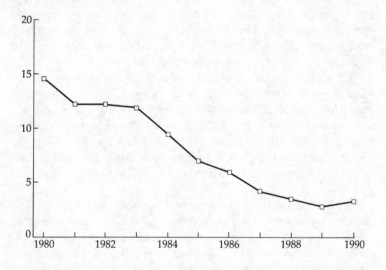

FIG. 6.3 Inflation differential between Italy and Germany (DPI) (per cent)
Source: EC Commission (1990).

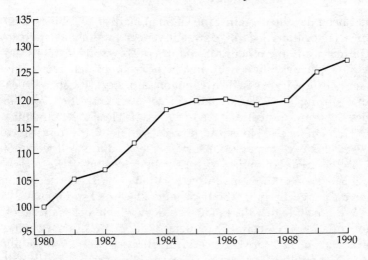

FIG. 6.4 Price index in Italy relative to Germany (CPI) expressed in common currency
Source: EC Commission (1990).

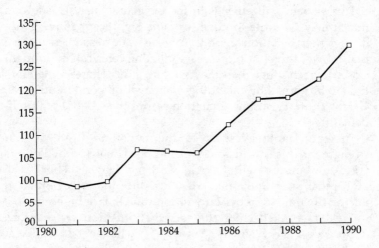

FIG. 6.5 Unit labour costs in Italy relative to OECD expressed in common currency
Source: EC Commission (1990).

not been devalued against the German mark at all. This has led to a continuous loss of competitiveness for Italy relative to Germany and the other EMS countries. This is made clear from Fig. 6.4, which shows the Italian price index relative to the German one (expressed in common currency). It can be seen that during the 1980s Italian prices (after correction for the devaluations of the lira) have increased by close to 30% relative to German prices. Note also the acceleration of this trend since 1988. This is certainly an unsustainable situation as it jeopardizes the competitiveness of the Italian economy. The strong deterioration of the competitive position of the Italian economy (as measured by unit labour costs) is illustrated in Fig. 6.5.

We conclude that the gradual strategy which makes the steps towards the final stage of monetary union conditional on the existence of full convergence of inflation rates is a dangerous one. Not only is it a very slow one; more importantly it may fail to lead to full convergence. There is no guarantee that the convergence of inflation rates that was achieved at the end of the 1980s in the EMS can be improved significantly. In 1990–91 we may in fact have reached the best possible convergence of inflation rates.

This evidence, together with the theoretical analysis, suggests that it may be futile to hope for more significant convergence during the transition period. There is little reason to believe that in two, three, or more years inflation rates can be brought closer to each other than they were in 1991. There is therefore little to be gained by extending the transition period until 1999. On the contrary, a slow transition carries the risk of being self-defeating.

There is another aspect to the transition problem that strengthens this conclusion. This has been analysed by Walters (1986), and more recently by Giavazzi and Spaventa (1990). The high-inflation country that tries to reduce its rate of inflation during the transition period will continue to face high nominal interest rates, reflecting the fact that inflation expectations decline only very slowly. Since the exchange rate is fixed, however, this creates an incentive for short-term capital inflows. True, rational economic agents will expect that the high-inflation country may be forced to devalue its currency in the future. They may, however, attach a low probability to this happening in the near future. As a result, they may find it attractive to invest funds in short-term, high-yielding assets of the high-inflation country.

This capital inflow now tends to increase the domestic money stock of the high-inflation country, making it all the more difficult to follow an anti-inflationary policy. Thus, in this view there is a destabilizing element in the slow transition process, which may be self-defeating. This has become a more acute problem since countries like Italy abolished capital controls in 1990. It leads to the conclusion that little can be gained from stretching the transition process. Too long a transition process carries the danger that the final objective will not be reached.

Why have the European authorities chosen the gradual high-risk transition process towards EMU? One possible explanation is that some countries lack a commitment to the ultimate objective of EMU, and therefore favour a process that postpones the introduction of EMU. Until recently, the British government was seen to be the obstructing force. The reasons were mostly political and were based on a perceived loss of sovereignty. More recently, the German government has shown some hesitation. The basis of this hesitation is an economic one, to which we now turn our attention.

4. The Incentives of the Low-Inflation Country

The Barro–Gordon model allows us to understand why the low-inflation country has little incentive to move to EMU. As was made clear in Fig. 5.10, Germany has nothing to gain (in terms of inflation and unemployment) from joining a union with high-inflation countries. Even if it insists, and succeeds, in obtaining a European central bank which is a copy of the Bundesbank, Germany still does not gain anything. It will face the same inflation equilibrium. All the gains are for the high-inflation countries.

More importantly, even if the European central bank had the same preferences regarding inflation and unemployment as the Bundesbank has, it is quite possible that the inflation equilibrium in the EMU would be higher than the one which prevailed in Germany prior to EMU. The reason has to do with structural

differences between union members, which would give incentives to the Eurofed policy-makers to inflate more, even if they
were as 'hard-nosed' as the Bundesbank policy-makers. We
illustrate this case in Fig. 6.6. We assume that the natural
unemployment rate (NAIRU) in Italy is higher than in Germany.
As a result, the NAIRU in the union as a whole is higher than in
Germany. The Eurofed policy-makers are assumed to be as
'hard-nosed' as the German policy-makers. We represent this
by drawing identical indifference curves for the Eurofed
authorities as for the German monetary authorities. The left-
hand panel represents Germany prior to the EMU. The right-
hand panel represents EMU. Given our assumption that the
NAIRU is higher in the EMU than in Germany, the inflation
equilibrium will be higher in the EMU. It is obtained at point *F*.
The EMU has an inflationary bias, not because the Eurofed
authorities are softer on inflation than the German authorities,
but because the higher natural unemployment rate in the EMU
forces them into a higher inflation path which is consistent

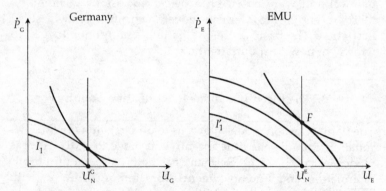

FIG. 6.6 Inflation equilibrium in Germany and EMU (same policy
preferences of Bundesbank and Eurofed)

with economic agents' expectations of how a higher NAIRU
affects the authorities' behaviour.[7]

The previous theoretical discussion assumes that the natural
rate of unemployment is lower in Germany than in the other

[7] Note that we assume here that the EMU authorities do not rescale their
preferences. With rescaling, the EMU authorities, realizing that the natural

EMS countries. Is there evidence for this? Table 6.1 presents some rough indicators of the natural rate of unemployment in the EMS countries. We take a ten-year average of the unemployment rates in these countries (1981–90) as our measure of the natural rate of unemployment. Admittedly, this can only be considered an approximation. It is striking, however, that Germany has the lowest unemployment rate of all the EMS countries. If the figures in Table 6.1 are good measures of the natural unemployment rates, there is reason to believe that a Eurofed, even if it consisted of individuals as 'hard-nosed' as the German authorities today, would have an incentive to produce more inflation.

TABLE 6.1. *Average unemployment rates during 1981–1990*

Belgium	10.7
Denmark	7.6
France	9.2
Germany	6.3
Ireland	16.5
Italy	9.6
Netherlands	10.2
UK	9.7

Source: EC Commission (1990: 223).

We conclude that the low-inflation country has no incentive to join a monetary union with high-inflation countries, because there is a strong probability that it would end up with more inflation without any gain in terms of unemployment. This is probably the major factor behind Germany's efforts to postpone the introduction of a European central bank. (Note, however, that countries may have other reasons to join a monetary union. For example, they may consider the other gains of a monetary union, which we discussed in Chapter 3, worthwhile or they may pursue political objectives by joining a union.)

unemployment rate has increased, attach the same utility loss to a *deviation* of the observed unemployment rate from the new NAIRU, as the utility loss from the same *deviation* relative to the lower NAIRU. Graphically this implies that the indifference curve I_1 corresponds to the same utility level as I'_1.

There is one way in which the incentives for the German monetary authorities to join EMU can be improved. That is to ensure that the individuals who would run the Eurofed are even more 'hard-nosed' about inflation than the German authorities themselves. (This can also be seen in Fig. 6.6. If the European authorities have flatter indifference curves, then a lower inflation equilibrium will result.) Put differently, if the German monetary authorities are forced to accept EMU, they will probably insist on having a Eurofed that attaches more importance to price stability than the Bundesbank does today. This brings us to the issue of how to devise a European central bank. This is taken up in the next chapter.

5. The Parallel Currency Approach to Monetary Unification

The parallel currency approach to monetary unification has been hotly debated in the academic literature. The Delors Report came out against this approach, so that the issue of whether this was a useful alternative seemed to be buried. However, in 1990, the British government formally proposed the use of a parallel currency, the hard ECU, as an alternative road to monetary unification in Europe. What seemed to have become a purely academic issue became an item on the agenda of practical men.

The idea of using a parallel currency to force monetary integration is not a new one. Numerous academic proposals have been formulated. One of the best known is the 'All Saints' Day Manifesto' published in *The Economist* on 1 November 1975.

The basic idea of the parallel currency approach is that a European currency which is made attractive enough will readily be used by economic agents, and in so doing drive the national currencies out of the market. At the end of the road we will have monetary union. One of the main intellectual attractions of this approach to monetary unification is that the movement and the speed towards EMU will be determined by the free choice of European citizens, and not by decisions taken by politicians and bureaucrats. In addition, the competition provided by this parallel currency will force the national monetary authorities to behave better. As a result, this strategy will have the interesting side-effect of reducing inflation.[8]

The experience with the ECU suggests that the mere existence of a parallel European currency is not sufficient to trigger a dynamics towards monetary union. In fact, the original drafters of the EMS hoped that the ECU would play this role. After more than ten years of existence it can now be said that the ECU has not fulfilled these expectations. The ECU has remained very marginal as a European currency. As a medium of exchange it is used very little. The great bulk of transactions in Europe are made using national currencies. Similarly, the ECU is used very little as a unit of account. Apart from the Community institutions few national agents (private and official) use the ECU as a unit of account. Some economists had predicted that the ECU would be used as an invoicing currency in international trade. However, the evidence suggests that this has not happened on a large scale. Today less than one per cent of international trade in the Community uses the ECU.[9]

More surprising is the fact that, despite high hopes, the ECU has not really become a major currency of denomination in the international bond markets. In the early 1980s there was a general expectation that the ECU could play a major role in the international bond markets. The reasoning behind this hope was that the basket definition of the ECU would be attractive for the small investor wishing to hedge against exchange risk.

Table 6.2 shows that the ECU has not become a major currency in the international bond markets.[10] At the end of 1989 only 4.4% of the outstanding *stock* of bonds issued in the international markets were denominated in ECU, a much smaller percentage than the dollar, the yen, the German mark,

[8] This aspect of the parallel currency approach is very much influenced by Hayek who developed the idea that competition in the creation of money leads to a lower inflation. See also Salin (1984). This book also contains an interesting chapter by Vaubel, who has been a leading advocate of free competition in the supply of money in Europe. See also Vaubel (1978) and (1990).

[9] See Jozzo (1989) for evidence. See also De Grauwe and Peeters (1989) and Lomax (1989).

[10] It should be stressed that these numbers overstate the importance of the ECU in the bond markets. The international (Euro-) bond market is only a small fraction of the total market in bonds, which includes the national bond markets. In the latter the ECU is almost never used. See Lomax (1989) on this.

TABLE 6.2. *The ECU in the international bond market*

Currency	Stock outstanding end of 1989 ($US bn.)	New issues in 1989 ($US bn.)
ECU	54.9	11.9
German mark	121.6	17.7
Yen	131.4	23.6
Pound sterling	81.6	21.3
Swiss franc	140.3	19.3
US dollar	565.9	127.7
Total (all currencies)	1,249.0	261.2

Source: BIS, *International Banking and Financial Market Developments*, Basle, Feb. 1991.

the Swiss franc, or the pound sterling. Similarly new issues in ECU during 1989 were equally small.

On the whole it is fair to conclude that the ECU has not become a major currency in Europe. It is not used as a medium of exchange and as a unit of account, nor is it a major investment vehicle.

The main reason for this failure of the ECU to perform its monetary role is that it has few natural advantages. Its basket definition may be attractive to small investors; it does not, however, give the ECU an advantage when used as a medium of exchange or a unit of account. In addition, since it contains many currencies that are subject to relatively large inflation, it has a handicap for economic agents living in low-inflation countries. It is very unlikely that the ECU, as it is presently defined, will ever be used freely by these economic agents to make domestic and international payments, or to invest.

From the experience of the ECU it follows that the parallel currency approach to EMU can only succeed if the ECU is made more attractive than it is today. Several proposals have been made to achieve this. The All Saints' Day Manifesto proposed to introduce an ECU which would be inflation-proof.[11] The UK

---

[11] For a discussion, see Fratianni and Peeters (1978). For other proposals to make the ECU more attractive, see Steinherr (1989).

government has recently presented a plan that would make the ECU more attractive by ensuring that it would never devalue against any of the national currencies. As a result, this 'hard' ECU would always be the strongest currency in Europe. This would also imply that the 'hard' ECU would cease to be a basket currency. It would really be a new ECU, defined in such a way that it would maintain its exchange rate fixed against the EC currency which appreciates most against the other currencies. According to the UK government, this would be sufficient to give the ECU an advantage, so that economic agents (if given the choice) would select that currency as a medium of exchange and a unit of account.[12]

Whether such a hard ECU stands any chance of displacing national currencies as a medium of exchange and a unit of account is very doubtful. There is a substantial amount of empirical evidence suggesting that such an outcome is very unlikely. In a well-known study of hyperinflation Cagan (1950) found that, with the exception of the German hyperinflation of 1923, for all the other seven hyperinflations there was no significant replacement of the domestic currency by other (low-inflation) currencies. Barro (1972) estimated that the fraction of transactions made by substitute moneys (or even barter) during hyperinflations was only 5% (see also Klein (1978)). This empirical evidence suggests that a hard ECU would have little chance of displacing national currencies that are subject to at most 10% inflation a year. If history is any guide, one would need truly dramatically high inflations in member states of the Community to lead to significant currency substitution.

The reason why currency substitution is so low may have something to do with a basic feature of money. As Tobin once noted, money, like a language, is a public good. The utility of money for an individual derives from the fact that others also use this money. Money used by one individual is of no use. This contrasts with a private good: the utility an individual

---

[12] The UK government presented a formal draft treaty embodying these ideas (see HM Treasury (1990)). It is unclear whether this proposal represents simply a strategy to postpone monetary union in Europe, or whether it reflects a genuine belief on the part of the UK authorities about the merits of the parallel currency approach.

derives from its use is independent of the fact that others also use the same good.

The public-good nature of money now implies that switching to a new currency does not come about easily by private initiative. Individuals may have an incentive to use another currency. They will, however, have to convince many other people to make the same switch before it becomes profitable to them. In other words, there is a co-ordination problem which drastically raises the transaction cost of switching to another currency.[13] Private initiative will generally fail to organize such a switch, except when the benefits of doing so increase dramatically (e.g. during hyperinflation). In order to organize such a switch to a new currency, government action (e.g. a monetary reform) will be necessary.

This co-ordination problem of a switch to a new currency is very similar to the one that arises in the selection of standards. For example, the QWERTY keyboard is certainly inferior to other keyboards. The superiority of these other keyboards, however, has proved to be insufficient to displace the QWERTY keyboard.[14]

In order to make the hard ECU a real alternative to national currencies, a minimal requirement would be that the national governments declare the hard ECU legal tender alongside the national currency, so that citizens could, for example, choose to pay their taxes in ECUs instead of in national currency. A failure of the national governments to accept the ECU in payment of tax liabilities would make it unlikely that citizens would want to use ECUs spontaneously.

If the legal-tender quality of the hard ECU is accepted by the national authorities, however, new problems arise. Take the problem of the shopkeepers. Since two currencies would circulate side by side, shopkeepers would have to quote two sets of prices. However, the ECU exchange rates of national currencies vary day by day in the market (given that there are bands of fluctuations around the central rates). Suppose these shopkeepers quote ECU prices using the central rates. In that case consumers will have an incentive to use the currency which is the weaker in the market. For example, if in the foreign

---

[13] See Klein (1978) on this problem.   [14] See David (1985).

exchange market the national currency drops below the central rate against the ECU, consumers have an incentive to use the national currency to make their payments. The opposite would occur if the ECU is weak. (Note that this is nothing but an application of *Gresham's law*, which says that bad money drives out good money. In Box 9 we develop this idea further.) Shopkeepers can avoid the problem of being paid in the 'bad' money by using market rates to quote ECU prices. The trouble with that solution, however, is that they would have to change the price tags very frequently, thereby reducing the usefulness of the ECU.

The government would essentially have the same problem as the shopkeepers. Since taxpayers would be free to pay their taxes using the national currency or the ECU, the government would have to publish the conversion rate at which taxes could be paid in ECU. If the government published a fixed exchange rate (say the central rate) the Gresham's law problem arises. Taxpayers would use the weak currency to fulfil their tax obligations. Alternatively, the government could publish variable rates. These would have to be adjusted on a daily basis. Again this is not a very attractive feature of this monetary system.

The parallel currency approach brings us back to the problems of a bimetallic standard. Due to the operation of Gresham's law, this monetary standard is highly unstable. In such a system there is no guarantee that the ECU would displace the national currency. It could be the other way around.

The only way to avoid problems stemming from the operation of Gresham's law consists in eliminating the fixity of the exchange rates in the EMS. This, however, would certainly be a step backwards. It also implies that the parallel currency approach, which is supposed to be a strategy leading to monetary union, first has to undo the degree of monetary integration achieved in the EMS, so as to be able to move forwards. This is certainly a high-risk approach to monetary unification. It, therefore, also has little chance of ever being applied.

BOX 9   THE PARALLEL CURRENCY AND GRESHAM'S LAW

It is useful to illustrate how Gresham's law will operate when a parallel currency, say the ECU, is declared legal tender alongside the national currency. Call the national currency the franc.

Assume that the central rate of the ECU in terms of the franc is equal to 5. Since the ECU and the franc are legal tender, shopkeepers will have to quote a franc price and an ECU price for their products. Thus, consumers can for example buy bread worth 10 francs by presenting 10 francs or 2 ECUs.

Suppose now that in the exchange market the ECU increases to 5.1. (This would still keep the ECU–franc rate within the permissible band of fluctuation.) It will then be in the interest of the consumers to sell the ECUs they hold for transaction purposes in the foreign exchange market, in order to obtain francs. For example, if a consumer was holding 1,000 ECUs for transaction purposes, he would obtain 5,100 francs in the foreign exchange market. He would then use francs in the shops (where he could buy 1,000 ECUs worth of goods with 5,000 francs). Thus, converting his 1,000 ECUs to francs in the foreign exchange market, and using the francs to buy goods and services, allows him to make a profit of 100 francs.

This arbitrage activity by consumers is nothing but an application of Gresham's law. The weak currency will be used in transactions, whereas the strong one is not used to make payments. Paradoxically, Gresham's law predicts that a 'hard' ECU will not be used as a medium of exchange.

In order to avoid the operation of Gresham's law, the shopkeepers would have to quote their prices using the market rates to convert franc prices into ECU prices. Since these market rates are changing continuously, the shopkeepers would have to adjust the ECU prices of their products continuously (say daily).

Alternatively, they could fix the ECU prices of their products and adjust the franc prices continuously. It is clear that such a system would be extremely cumbersome, and that shopkeepers and consumers would have an incentive to use just one money.

The same problem arises for the government collecting taxes. Since taxpayers have the choice of paying taxes in francs or in ECUs, the government would have to publish official conversion rates. Suppose again that the conversion rate is 5 francs = 1 ECU. If the ECU increases in value in the foreign exchange market to, say, 5.1, taxpayers will sell their transaction balances of ECU for francs, and use the latter to pay their taxes.

The government can avoid this problem by adjusting the official conversion rate continuously so as to reflect the market exchange rate between the franc and the ECU. If it fixes the franc value of the taxes, the ECU value of these taxes will vary continuously. It is very unlikely that taxpayers will want to use the ECU in such circumstances.

7

A European Central Bank

1. Introduction

At the Maastricht summit meeting of December 1991 it was agreed that, at the latest in 1999, a European Cental Bank (ECB) will be set up, which will manage the ECU. It is not clear yet whether the ECU will then immediately displace the national currencies of those countries that participate in the monetary union, or whether it will circulate alongside these national currencies, albeit with 'irrevocably' fixed exchange rates. The Maastricht Treaty is ambivalent about which of the two regimes will prevail.

In this chapter it will first be shown that there are major differences between the two regimes. These differences are qualitative in nature and will require very different institutions. Secondly, assuming that in the final stage one European currency will have displaced the national currencies, we will analyse the question of how to devise a central bank for Europe that manages this European currency. The issue that will have to be dealt with is how this European central bank can be given incentives so that it performs at least as well as the central banks in low-inflation countries today. This is an important issue, for as we have argued in the previous chapter, the willingness of the low-inflation countries to join a full monetary union is very much dependent on how inflation-prone the European central bank is likely to be.

2. Irrevocably Fixed Exchange Rates or a Common Currency

Let us first analyse how these two regimes can be introduced in the final stage of the EMU. We concentrate first on the introduction of the common currency.

A *common currency* can be introduced in two ways. One consists in announcing that on a particular day national currencies will be abolished and be replaced by the European currency, say the ECU. Thus on that day, European citizens will have to convert their holdings of national currencies into the ECU, at a given conversion rate. The ECU will then be legal tender in all countries.

An alternative, and equivalent, approach consists in starting with a *monetary reform* in the following way. All national currencies are converted into new national currencies so that they are all at par, i.e. one German mark = one guilder = one French franc = one lira, etc. This could be achieved by using the ECU rates to convert each currency. Thus on conversion day, the Germans present 2.04 old marks and receive one new mark, the French present 6.95 old francs and receive one new franc, the Italians present 1,540 old lire in exchange for one new lira. The new national currencies then have the same worth as one ECU. When this is done, the national currencies are declared legal tender in each country. This means that a German shopkeeper must accept guilders, or francs, or lire in payment. Since all these currencies are at par, he has no difficulty in doing this. He can also quote just one price for his products. The mark price is exactly the same as the guilder price, the franc price, the lira price.[1]

When we have reached this situation, we can say that the national currencies become perfect substitutes, i.e. residents of each country will not really care whether they carry marks, francs, guilders, etc. in their wallets. There will also be no need to have organized exchange markets any more. Note that this is the regime prevailing between Belgium and Luxemburg today.

It is easy to see that this monetary reform is equivalent to the introduction of a common currency. We can call the new values of the national currencies one ECU. In what follows we will consider the regime in which national currencies circulate at

---

[1] It will be clear here that the conversion operation leading to currencies that are traded at par is essential. If such conversion is not done, the shopkeeper will be forced to establish as many different price lists as there are national currencies when each currency becomes legal tender. This will lead to great practical problems. It may also lead to refusals to accept payment in foreign currencies.

par and are legal tender in each country to be equivalent to the regime of a common currency.

The common currency regime just described is very different from an 'irrevocably fixed' exchange rate system. Suppose that in the final stage, the national authorities announce that, from now on, the exchange rates are 'irrevocably fixed' at the rates that prevail at that moment. Suppose also that in this regime each currency maintains its sole legal-tender status domestically. Such a regime of irrevocably fixed exchange rates is qualitatively very different from a regime with a common currency. The reasons are the following.

First, as was stressed in the previous chapter, in the absence of a legal-tender status of foreign currencies, residents of one country will not easily use foreign currencies in domestic transactions. The evidence about countries in hyperinflation indicates that the substitution of foreign currencies is very difficult, even if the inflation to which the national currency is subjected is extremely high.

Secondly, irrevocably fixed exchange rates between national currencies that continue to be used in each country, inevitably lead to the problem of the credibility of the fixity of the exchange rate. It is very likely that doubts will exist about the 'irrevocable' fixity of these exchange rates. This will make it difficult to equalize interest rates between the countries. If there is some doubt that one currency may be devalued in the future, the interest rate in the country involved will have to increase relative to the other currencies.

This has important implications for the workings of the interbank markets. Domestic banks whose liabilities are to a large extent expressed in local currency will find it unattractive to use the foreign currencies as vehicle currencies in their interbank market dealings. The uncertainty about future exchange rate developments and the interest rate differentials that ensue, will give an incentive to French, German, and Italian banks to deal in the franc, mark, and lira interbank markets to settle their short-term claims and liabilities. In other words, the degree of currency substitutability in the interbank market will also be limited.

Thirdly, the existence of separate currencies each having legal-tender status in its own country, albeit with 'irrevocably fixed' exchange rates, will not eliminate the need to use the foreign exchange market. Foreign European currencies will have to be bought and sold through these markets. This will involve transactions costs. In Chapter 3 we gave some evidence about the possible size of these transactions costs. We noted that in the case of the guilder and the German mark these transactions costs were still around 0.5%, and not much lower than in other exchange markets, despite the fact that the guilder/mark exchange rate is close to what one can call an 'irrevocably' fixed exchange rate, i.e. the guilder/mark exchange rate has not been changed since 1983, and the band of fluctuation has been reduced to about 1%.

As a result of these transactions costs, there is little direct substitutability between the guilder and the mark. Dutch residents continue to do the overwhelming amount of their domestic transactions in guilders, and German residents do the same in their own country.

We conclude that an 'irrevocably fixed' exchange rate regime is fundamentally different from a regime with a common currency which has displaced the national currencies. Therefore, the institutions that will be needed to support these two systems are quite different. We discuss these institutional differences in the following sections.

3. Institutional Implications of an 'Irrevocably Fixed' Exchange Rate System

The institutional aspects of the two regimes, i.e. separate national currencies with irrevocably fixed exchange rates and a common currency are very different. To show this, let us first see how the regime with separate currencies with fixed exchange rates can work.

In essence this fixed exchange rate system is just a further development of the present EMS regime. The difference would be that the exchange rates are declared to be irrevocably fixed instead of being subject to realignments. Some of the problems of the EMS would also apply to this regime. In particular the uncertainty in the irrevocable fixity of the exchange rates would still be present.

In principle, however, this regime does not need a common central bank. It can function very much like the present EMS, in which one country plays a dominant role. In other words the regime can function when one country fixes its money stock, and the others peg their currency to the centre country. (The reader is referred to Chapter 5, Fig. 5.1, where it was shown that in this regime the centre country fixes its money stock. This determines the interest rate in the centre country and uniquely determines the interest rate in the peripheral countries by the interest-parity condition. The centre country is an anchor for the whole system.)

As was mentioned in the chapter on the workings of the EMS, this asymmetric system has advantages. It also has its share of problems, both political and economic, which leads to the issue of its sustainability. The problems of monetary control that arise in an asymmetric system (and which were analysed in the chapter on the EMS) are likely to lead to conflicts about the kind of monetary policy to be followed for the whole system. For example, during a recession originating in the peripheral countries, these will find that the monetary policies they have to endure are inappropriate. Pressures on the centre country will certainly be exerted. These conflicts of interests will have to be dealt with in one way or another.

The preceding discussion also suggests that an 'irrevocably fixed' exchange rate system in which one country dominates the monetary policy-making may not survive in the long run. Too much conflict will exist about the appropriate monetary policies for the system as a whole. Peripheral countries, especially if they are similar in size to the centre country (as is the case in the present EMS), may not be willing to subject their national interests to the survival of the system. The 'irrevocable fixity' of the exchange rates is unlikely to remain so. We conclude that this model of the future monetary union in Europe is not a stable one.

What about the 'irrevocably fixed' exchange rate system with a common European central bank?

Suppose that in the final stage the European Central Bank (ECB) takes over from the national central banks. Assume that the national currencies maintain their (exclusive) legal-tender status domestically, and that the exchange rates are 'irrevocably fixed'. How could such a system be made to work?

It will now be necessary that the ECB sets an objective for

the money stock in the whole system, and translates this into objectives for each national currency. We represent this set of objectives in Fig. 7.1 by the vertical lines of the money supply M_1 and M_2. In general, such an institutional environment will not avoid pressures in the foreign exchange market. To see this, suppose that there are different shocks in the money demand equations in the two countries. Such differences might occur because of different business cycles in the two countries. We represent these differences by an upward shift in the money demand function of country 2.

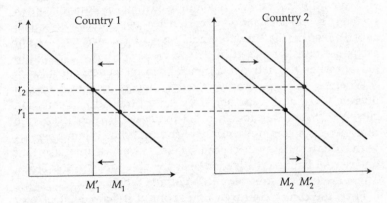

FIG. 7.1 Fixed exchange rate regime with common central bank

This (asymmetric) shock will tend to push the interest rate of country 2 upwards, so that a movement of liquidity from country 1 to country 2 is set in motion. This movement will be reflected by sales of currency 1 in the exchange market, and purchases of currency 2. The ECB will have to intervene by selling currency 2 against currency 1 to maintain the fixity of the exchange rate, thereby increasing the money stock of country 2 and reducing it in country 1. We represent this by the shifts of the money stock lines.

If confidence in the fixity of the exchange rate is strong, this mechanism will generally not lead to problems. Problems may arise if these movements in the foreign exchange market lead to doubts about the 'irrevocable' fixity of the exchange rates. We conclude that, even if this system operates with one European central bank, it does not avoid the credibility problem. The issue of the long-run sustainability of this system arises. If one wants to avoid these problems, it is inevitable that one moves to a regime with a common currency.

4. Institutional Implications of a Common Currency

In a regime with a common currency the institutions that will be needed for monetary control will have to be very different from those that are observed in fixed exchange rate regimes. As shown earlier, a system of a common currency is equivalent to a system where the national currencies have become perfect substitutes. Let us therefore analyse how the system of fixed exchange rates, analysed in the previous section, will have to operate when the national currencies become perfect substitutes.

Whereas an 'irrevocably' fixed exchange rate system can operate without a common European central bank, a common currency system cannot. In order to show this, let us assume that there is a common currency, and that the system operates with different national central banks. Let us assume also that one central bank is the leader (as is the case today in the EMS). There are two reasons why this will not work.

First, the centre country cannot control its money stock any more. Direct substitutability of the two national moneys means that the national money demand functions become unstable, i.e. small disturbances lead to large shifts in these demand functions. Suppose, as before, that a boom originates in the peripheral country. This will shift the money demand function in that country. The slight increase in the interest rate in the peripheral country now triggers an increase in the demand for the centre's currency. Thus, there will be an upward shift in the money demand function leading to an increase in the interest rate of the centre. The centre country could of course peg its interest rate. However, this would not solve the problem. In that case the domestic money stock would have to increase. We conclude that in a regime of common currency (perfect substitutability of national currencies) the centre country loses its monetary control.

A second reason why the institutional arrangements of a

common currency regime will have to be very different from the one prevailing under a fixed exchange rate regime has to do with the lack of discipline that is imposed on the peripheral countries.[2] In the common currency regime where national central banks would continue to exist, countries will have a strong incentive to oversupply their own currency. The reason is the following. Each country can now supply a currency that will be legal tender domestically and in all the other countries. For each unit of domestic money issued, the country gains one unit of seigniorage revenue. The effect on inflation, however, is spread over all the countries. Thus the country that issues money gets all the benefits, whereas the cost is spread over the whole system. This is a sure recipe for over-issuing national moneys. In the fixed exchange rate regime there is a strong brake on this over-issue, because the country that does this quickly loses international reserves through the sales of the domestic currency in the foreign exchange market. This brake is absent in the common currency regime because exchange markets have disappeared in that regime.

It should also be noted that the incentive for over-issuing the national currency is stronger for smaller countries than for larger ones. A small country that issues one unit of the domestic currency gets one unit of seigniorage income, while the effect on the system's inflation (and thus on the domestic inflation) is small. This is much less the case for the larger country.

The preceding discussion implies that a common currency regime can work only if a common central bank takes over the responsibilities of the national central banks.

5. The Design of the European Central Bank

In the previous chapter we deduced the proposition that the incentive for the low-inflation country to join a monetary union with high-inflation countries is low. There is nothing to be gained for the low-inflation country in terms of inflation and unemployment. All the gains are for the high-inflation countries.

This strong asymmetry in incentives is very important in the

---

[2] See Krugman (1990).

design of the European central bank. It means that there is only one way for the low-inflation country to agree to move to the final stage. The condition is that the European central bank is as 'hard-nosed' about inflation as the low-inflation country's own central bank. Failure to devise such an institutional copy of the low-inflation central bank will lead to a situation where the low-inflation country refuses to take the final step to EMU.

In fact, as was shown in the previous chapter, the problem is probably worse in the present context of European monetary union. The natural rate of unemployment happens to be higher in the high-inflation countries than in Germany. This leads to a fear that even if the future European central bank is institutionally a copy of the Bundesbank, it will face much stronger pressures to be soft on inflation than the Bundesbank today. As a result, the low-inflation country (Germany) is likely to insist that the European central bank, more than the Bundesbank itself, gives an overriding priority to keeping inflation low.

There is now a widespread consensus among economists that two conditions have to be satisfied to ensure that the Eurofed will pursue non-inflationary policies. These conditions must be given a formal expression in the statutes of the European central bank.[3]

First, the statutes of the ECB should explicitly declare that the only macroeconomic objective of the European monetary policy is price stability. Thus, reference to high employment as an objective of monetary policy should be avoided.

Secondly, the ECB should be institutionally independent of the political authorities (including the European Commission and the European parliament). Political independence is crucial to ensure that budget deficits of the national and European governments will not be financed by printing money. In an institutional environment where the central bank is an appendix of the ministry of finance (as is the case in many, if not most, countries in the world) it is inevitable that the central bank will be forced to finance the budget deficits. This is the surest way to produce inflation.

There is a lot of evidence to the effect that the political independence of central banks matters to keep inflation low.

---

[3] For a recent discussion of these conditions see Manfred Neumann (1990).

There have been studies by Bade and Parkin (1985), Demopoulos, Katsimbris, and Miller (1987), and more recently by Alesina (1989) showing that central banks that are politically independent tend to produce less inflation than central banks that have to take orders from the government.

The striking fact is that the statutes of the European Central Bank, proposed in the Maastricht Treaty, contain the two conditions spelled out above. This is illustrated by the following articles of the Treaty:

'The primary objective of the European System of Central Banks shall be to maintain price stability.'

'When exercising the powers and carrying out the tasks and duties conferred upon them by this Treaty (. . .), neither the ECB nor a national central bank, nor any member of their decision-making bodies shall seek or take instructions from Community institutions or bodies, from any Government of a Member State or from any other body.'

And the Treaty has the following sentence:

'The Treaty prohibits overdraft facilities or any other type of credit facility with the European Central Bank or with the national central banks to Community institutions or bodies, Central Governments, regional or local authorities, public authorities, (. . .) and the purchase directly from them of debt instruments.'

This seems to confirm that the drafters of the statutes of the ECB have understood the basic asymmetry in the incentives of countries to join the EMU. As a result, they have taken pains to ensure that the ECB, at least on paper, will be an institution akin to the Bundesbank. It might even be said that the language used by the drafters of the statutes of the ECB is tougher on inflation and political independence than the statutes of the Bundesbank.

The question that arises here is whether the explicit recognition in the statutes of the ECB of political independence and of price stability as the primary objective of monetary policy is sufficient (it is certainly necessary) to guarantee an inflation-proof ECB. One can express doubts about this. The individuals who are going to make monetary policy are subject to social and cultural influences. Some come from countries where abhorrence *vis-à-vis* inflation is not as intense as in Germany. They may therefore act differently from the individuals sitting on the board of the Bundesbank, even if the statutes of the ECB have been copied from the Bundesbank statutes. In addition, as was mentioned earlier, differences in the natural rate of unemployment may make them more prone than the representatives of Germany to be soft on inflation.

Some economists (e.g. Manfred Neumann (1990) and Roland Vaubel (1989)) have proposed incentive schemes for the ECB policy-makers that would make it more likely that they pursue non-inflationary policies. One such scheme consists in paying the members of the board a fixed nominal salary, or even to reduce their salary for every point of inflation. These schemes may help, but are unlikely to eliminate completely the risk that the ECB will not be as inflation-conscious as the Bundesbank today.

6. Conclusion

In this chapter we have argued that the only viable form of a monetary union is one where a common currency has displaced the national currencies, and where one European central bank conducts monetary policy in the union. A system where national currencies maintain their domestic legal tender and whose exchange rates are 'irrevocably fixed' will suffer from a credibility problem, and therefore will not be robust in the long run.

Although the only viable system requires a common currency managed by a common central bank, this system is not without its problems. The inflationary discipline of the system will depend on what this common central bank does, and on its reputation. Despite the fact that on paper the ECB is as tough on inflation as the Bundesbank, doubts will exist for quite some time about the inflationary discipline that this institution can impose in Europe. These doubts are the single most important stumbling-block on the road towards EMU.

8

Fiscal Policies in Monetary Unions

1. Introduction

The traditional theory of optimum currency areas, which was discussed in Chapter 1, offers interesting insights about the conduct of national fiscal policies in a monetary union. In this chapter we start out by developing these ideas. We then challenge this theory by introducing issues of credibility and sustainability of fiscal policies.

The analysis of this chapter will allow us to answer questions such as:

● What is the role of fiscal policy in a monetary union?
● How independent can national fiscal policies be?
● Does a monetary union increase or reduce fiscal discipline? What rules, if any, should be used to restrict national fiscal policies?

2. Fiscal Policies and the Theory of Optimum Currency Areas

In order to analyse what the theory of optimum currency areas has to say about the conduct of fiscal policies, it is useful to start from the example of an asymmetric demand shock as developed in Chapter 1. Suppose again that European consumers shift their demand in favour of German products at the expense of French products. We reproduce the figure of Chapter 1 here (Fig. 8.1). What are the fiscal policy implications of this disturbance?

Suppose first that France and Germany, being members of the same monetary union, have also centralized a substantial

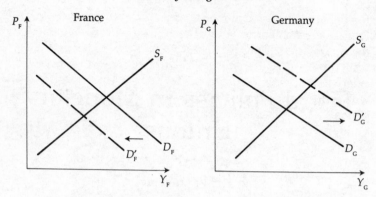

FIG. 8.1 Asymmetric shock in France and Germany

part of their national budgets to the central European authority. In particular, let us assume that the social security system is organized at the European level, and that income taxes are also levied by the European government.

It can now be seen that the centralized budget will work as a shock absorber. In France output declines and unemployment tends to increase. This has a double effect on the European budget. The income taxes collected by the European government in France decline, whereas unemployment benefit payments by the European authorities increase. Exactly the opposite occurs in Germany. There, output increases and unemployment declines. As a result, tax revenues collected by the European government in Germany increase, while European government spending in Germany declines. Thus, the centralized European budget automatically redistributes income from Germany to France, thereby softening the social consequences of the demand shift for France.

Consider now what would happen if France and Germany form a monetary union without centralizing their government budgets. It can easily be demonstrated that the negative demand shock in France will lead to an increase in the French government budget deficit, because tax receipts decline while unemployment benefit payments by the French government increase. The French government will have to increase its borrowing. In Germany we have the reverse. The German government budget experiences increasing surpluses (or declining deficits). If capital markets work efficiently, the need for the French government to borrow can easily be accommodated by the increasing supply of savings coming from Germany.

In this case of decentralized budgets, France increases its external debt which will have to be serviced in the future. This will reduce the degrees of freedom of future French fiscal policies. This contrasts with the case where the national budgets are centralized: in such a system, France will not have to face such external debt problems, as German residents automatically transfer income to France. They will not necessarily be repaid for their generosity.

It should also be stressed that the size of these budgetary effects very much depends on the degree of wage and price flexibility and/or labour mobility. If these are large, the automatic transfer from Germany (or in the second case, the French budget deficit) will be low. If, for example, labour mobility between France and Germany is high, there will be little unemployment in France, so that unemployment benefit payments are correspondingly low.

The theory of optimum currency areas leads to the following implications for fiscal policies in monetary unions (see Kenen (1969)). First, it is desirable to centralize a significant part of the national budgets to the European level. A centralized budget allows countries (and regions) that are hit by negative shocks to enjoy automatic transfers, thereby reducing the social costs of a monetary union. This was also a major conclusion of the influential MacDougall Report, published in 1977. The drafters of that report argued that monetary union in Europe would have to be accompanied by a significant centralization of budgetary power in Europe (more precisely a centralization of the unemployment benefit systems). Failure to do so would impose great social strains and endanger monetary union.

Secondly, if such a centralization of the national government budgets in a monetary union is not possible (as appears to be the case in the context of European monetary union), national fiscal policies should be used in a flexible way. That is, when countries are hit by negative shocks, they should be allowed to let the budget deficit increase through the built-in (or automatic) budgetary stabilizers (declining government revenues, increasing social outlays).

This requirement that fiscal policies respond flexibly to negative shocks also implies that a substantial autonomy should be reserved for these national fiscal policies. In the logic of the optimum currency area theory, countries lose an instrument of policy (the exchange rate) when they join the union. If there is no centralized budget which automatically redistributes income, countries have no instrument at their disposal to absorb the effects of these negative shocks.[1] The fiscal policy instrument is the only one left.

This theory about how fiscal policies should be conducted in a monetary union has been heavily criticized recently. This criticism is not directed at the first conclusion, i.e. that it is desirable to centralize a significant part of the national budgets in a monetary union. The criticism has been formulated against the second conclusion, which calls for flexibility and autonomy of national government budgets in monetary unions, when the degree of budgetary centralization is limited. To this criticism we now turn.

3. Sustainability of Government Budget Deficits

The major problem with the previous analysis is the underlying assumption that governments can create budget deficits to absorb negative shocks without leading to problems of sustainability of these deficits. As many Western European countries have experienced during the 1980s, however, government budget deficits quickly lead to such problems.

The sustainability problem can be formulated as follows. A budget deficit leads to an increase in government debt which will have to be serviced in the future. If the interest rate on the government debt exceeds the growth rate of the economy, a debt dynamics is set in motion which leads to an ever-increasing government debt relative to GDP. This becomes unsustainable, requiring corrective action.

We have already encountered this debt dynamics problem in

---

[1] We assume here that wages are inflexible and that labour mobility is non-existent.

Chapter 1, where we derived the following government budget constraint:

$$b = (g - t) + (r - x)b - \dot{m} \tag{1}$$

where b = the government debt, g = government spending (exclusive of interest payments), t = tax revenues, x = the growth rate of GDP, r = the interest rate on the debt, and $\dot{m}$ is the revenue from issuing money; b, g, t, and $\dot{m}$ are expressed as ratios to GDP.

As shown in Chapter 1 the debt to GDP ratio (b) increases indefinitely if the interest rate exceeds the growth rate of the economy $(r>x)$. The only way the government can stop this explosive debt dynamics is by creating sufficiently high primary surpluses $(t>g)$ or by increasing the rate of money creation. The latter option has been chosen by many Latin American countries during the 1980s. It has also led to hyperinflation in these countries.

The important message here is that if a country has accumulated sizeable deficits in the past, it will now have to run correspondingly large primary budget surpluses in order to prevent the debt to GDP ratio from increasing automatically. This means that the country will have to reduce spending and/or increase taxes.

It may be interesting here to present a few case-studies of the experience of European countries during the 1980s. We select Belgium, the Netherlands, and Italy. We present data on government budget deficits of these countries during the 1980s (see Fig. 8.2).

It can be seen that these countries allowed their budget deficits to increase significantly during the early part of the decade. This increase in government budget deficits came mainly as a response to the negative consequences of major recessions in these countries. The rest of the decade was characterized by strenuous attempts to contain the explosive debt situation that followed from these earlier policies. We show the evolution of the debt to GDP ratios in these countries during the decade in Fig. 8.3. Belgium and the Netherlands appear to have succeeded, after many years, in stabilizing the debt to GDP ratio. The level at which Belgium has been able to achieve this, however, is very high, making it quite impossible

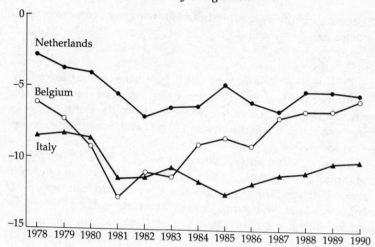

FIG. 8.2 General government budget balance (per cent of GDP)
Source: EC Commission (1990).

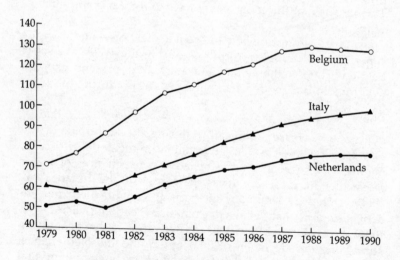

FIG. 8.3 Gross public debt (per cent of GDP)
Source: EC Commission (1990).

to use fiscal policies flexibly in the future if this country is hit by a negative demand shock again. Belgium and the Netherlands were able to stabilize their debt to GDP ratio by running substantial surpluses in the primary budget. These are shown in Table 8.1. At the end of 1990, Italy had not succeeded in stabilizing its debt to GDP ratio, because it failed to create the required primary budget surpluses. In addition, the constraints imposed by the EMS also made it impossible to have recourse to monetary financing.

These examples vividly demonstrate the limits to the use of fiscal policies to offset negative economic shocks. Such policies cannot be maintained for very long. The experience of these countries shows that large government budget deficits quickly lead to an unsustainable debt dynamics from which countries find it difficult to extricate themselves. The 'success' of Belgium

TABLE 8.1. *Budget balances, interest payments, and public debt (as per cent of GDP)*

	1988	1989	1990
(a) Budget balance			
Belgium	−6.6	−6.7	−5.8
Netherlands	−5.2	−5.2	−5.4
Italy	−10.9	−10.2	−10.1
(b) Interest payments			
Belgium	10.4	10.7	11.1
Netherlands	6.0	5.9	5.9
Italy	8.2	9.0	9.7
(c) Primary balance (a + b)			
Belgium	3.8	4.1	5.3
Netherlands	0.8	0.7	0.5
Italy	−2.7	−1.2	−0.4
(d) Public debt			
Belgium	132.2	129.9	129.4
Netherlands	77.4	77.6	77.8
Italy	96.1	98.9	100.9

Source: EC Commission (1990: 150).

in stabilizing the debt to GDP ratio by running primary budget surpluses during the second half of the 1980s came about after many years of spending cuts and tax increases.

The previous discussion also makes clear that fiscal policies are not the flexible instrument that the optimum currency theory has made us believe. The systematic use of this instrument quickly leads to problems of sustainability, which forces countries to run budget surpluses for a number of years. Put differently, when used once, it will not be possible to use these fiscal policies again until many years later.

This analysis of the sustainability of fiscal policies has led to a completely different view of the desirable fiscal policies of member states in a monetary union. This view was most vividly set out by the Delors Committee when it proposed that national fiscal policies, and in particular national government budget deficits, should be bound by strict rules.[2] This is a complete reversal of the traditional view based on the optimum currency area theory.

4. The Argument for Rules on Government Budget Deficits

The analysis of the sustainability problem leads to a very different view of the role of national fiscal policies in a monetary union.

The basic insight of this view is that a country that finds itself on an unsustainable path of increasing government debt creates negative externalities for the rest of the monetary union. A country that allows its debt to GDP ratio to increase continuously will have increasing recourse to the capital markets of the union, thereby driving the union interest rate upwards. This increase in the union interest rate in turn increases the burden of the government debts of the other countries. If the governments of these countries choose to stabilize their debt to GDP ratios, they will be forced to follow more restrictive fiscal policies. Thus, the unsustainable increase in the debt of one country forces the other countries to follow more deflationary

---

[2] See the Delors Report (1989).

policies. It will therefore be in the interest of these other countries that a control mechanism should exist restricting the size of budget deficits in the member countries.

There is a second externality that may appear here. The upward movement of the union interest rate, following the unsustainable fiscal policies of one member country, is likely to put pressure on the ECB. Countries that are hurt by the higher union interest rate may pressure the Eurofed to relax its monetary policy stance. Thus, unsustainable fiscal policies will interfere with the conduct of the European monetary policy. Again it may be in the interest of the members of the union to prevent such a negative externality to occur by imposing limits on the size of government budget deficits.

These arguments led the Delors Committee to propose binding rules on the size of national government budget deficits in a future monetary union. This proposal has led to serious criticism not only from the academic community but also from some EC countries' governments (in particular the UK).[3] The criticism has been twofold. One is theoretical and concerns the role of capital markets. The second has to do with the enforceability of such rules.

(a) The efficiency of private capital markets Implicit in the externality argument, there is an assumption that capital markets do not work properly. Let us now suppose that capital markets work efficiently, and ask the question what will happen when one country, say Italy, is on an unsustainable debt path. Does it mean that the union interest rate will increase, i.e. that the interest rate to be paid by German, Dutch, or French borrowers will equally increase? The answer is negative. If capital markets in the monetary union work efficiently, it will be recognized that the debt problem is an Italian problem. The market will attach a risk premium to Italian government debt. The German government, however, will not be affected by this. It will be able to borrow at a lower interest rate, because the lenders recognize that the risk inherent in German government bonds is lower than the risk involved in

---

[3] See e.g. Buiter and Kletzer (1990), van der Ploeg (1990), Wyplosz (1990), and von Hagen (1990).

buying Italian government debt instruments. Thus, if the capital markets work efficiently, there will be no externality. Other governments in the union will not suffer from the existence of a high Italian government debt. In addition, it does not make sense to talk about *the* union interest rate. If capital markets are efficient there will be different interest rates in the union, reflecting different risk premia on the government debt of the union members.

This is certainly a powerful argument. There is, however, a possibility that lenders will find it difficult to attach the correct risk premium to the Italian government debt. Let us analyse under what conditions this may happen. Suppose the lenders believe that in case of a serious debt crisis, i.e. an inability of the Italian government to service its debt, the other countries will step in to 'bail out' the Italian government. These countries may have an interest in doing so, because an Italian debt crisis may spill over to the rest of the financial system. For example, financial institutions in other countries may hold Italian government paper. A default by Italy may lead to defaults of these financial institutions, and may create a general debt crisis. To avoid this, the governments of other countries may decide to step in and buy up the Italian government paper. The realization that such an implicit bail-out guarantee exists will lower the risk premium on Italian government paper. Thus, the capital market fails to attach the correct price to risky Italian debt instruments.

One way to solve this problem consists in a solemn declaration of the members of the union that they will never bail out other member countries' governments. Such a 'no bail-out' clause was proposed at the Intergovernmental Conference in December 1990. Although such a declaration may help to resolve the problem, it is unlikely completely to eliminate it because it may not be fully credible. When an Italian debt crisis occurs, it will be in the interest of the other member countries to bail out the Italian government for the reasons given earlier. Thus, even if they have previously declared their intention not to intervene, they may very well decide to make an exception this time. The realization that this may happen in the future will hamper private lenders in correctly pricing the risk of Italian government debt.

(b) The enforcement of fiscal policy rules A second problem with the Delors Committee's proposal to impose binding rules on the size of government budget deficits has to do with the enforceability of these rules. Experience with such rules is that it is very difficult to enforce them. A recent example of such difficulties is the Gramm–Rudman legislation in the USA. In 1986 the US Congress approved a bill that set out explicit targets for the US Federal budget deficit. If these targets were not met, spending would automatically be cut across the board by a given percentage so as to meet the target. It can now be said that this approach with binding rules was not very successful. The US executive branch found all kinds of ways of circumventing this legislation. For example, some spending items were put 'off the budget'.

There is also evidence collected by von Hagen (1991) for the US states pointing in the same direction. Von Hagen found that those states that had constitutional limits on their budget deficits or on the level of their debt had frequent recourse to the technique of 'off-budgeting'. As a result, he found that the existence of constitutional rules had very little impact on the size of the states' budget deficits.

These criticisms against explicit rules for the conduct of fiscal policies in monetary unions have led to a reconsideration of the Delors Committee's proposal. In the Maastricht Treaty the idea of imposing strict rules was abandoned. Instead, member states of the monetary union are advised to avoid 'excessive' government budget deficits. The Commission will have the task of monitoring the budget deficits and the debt level of the national governments participating in the union. (Note, however, that strict budgetary rules have been imposed as a condition to enter the union).

5. Fiscal Discipline in Monetary Unions

An important issue relating to the need for rules on fiscal policies has to do with the way a monetary union affects the fiscal discipline of national governments in such a union. Proponents of rules have generally argued that a monetary union is likely to reduce the fiscal discipline of national governments. Adversaries of rules have argued the opposite.

In order to see clearly the different, and opposing, arguments it is useful to ask the question of how a monetary union may change the incentives of fiscal policy-makers, and in so doing, may affect budgetary discipline.

The issue of whether a monetary union increases or reduces the degree of fiscal discipline of countries joining the union has been hotly debated in the literature.[4] Broadly speaking there are two factors that are important here and that can lead to a change in the incentives of countries in regard to the size of their budget deficits when they join the union. The first one leads to less discipline, the second to more discipline.

The phenomenon that leads to incentives for larger budget deficits can be phrased as follows. When a sovereign country issues debt denominated in the domestic currency, the interest rate it will have to pay reflects a risk premium consisting of two components, the risk of default and the risk that the country will devalue its currency in the future. The latter can be completely eliminated by issuing debt in foreign currency. The risk premium then reflects the pure default risk. This also happens when a country joins a monetary union: the governments of the member states have to issue debt in what is equivalent to a 'foreign' currency. As a result, the risk premium (if any) will reflect the probability that the issuing government may not fully service its debt in the future.

As was indicated earlier, however, the lenders may have difficulties in correctly estimating this default risk because of an implicit bail-out guarantee that other members of the union extend. The possibility of a bail-out then gives an incentive to member states to issue unsustainable amounts of debt. A no-bail-out provision may not solve this problem because it is not likely to be credible. Even if the European authorities were solemnly to declare never to bail out member states, it is unlikely that they would stick to this rule if a member country faced the prospect of being unable to service its debt. Thus, the monetary union leads to excessive budget deficits of the member states. This 'moral hazard' problem also played an

---

[4] For a survey see Wyplosz (1990).

important role in the Delors Committee's proposal to impose rules on the size of the government budget deficits in a future European monetary union.

There is a second factor, however, which tends to reduce the incentive of member states of a monetary union to run excessive deficits. Countries who join the union reduce their ability to finance budget deficits by money creation. As a result, the governments of member states of a monetary union face a 'harder' budget constraint than sovereign nations. The latter are confronted with 'softer' budget constraints and therefore have a stronger incentive to run deficits.[5]

Which one of the two effects—the moral hazard or the no-monetization one—prevails is essentially an empirical question in that it depends on institutional features and on the incentives governments face. It is, therefore, useful to analyse the experience of member states in existing monetary unions and to compare this with the experience of sovereign nations. This is done in Table 8.2, where the average budget deficits of member states of existing monetary unions are presented together with the average of the budget deficits of the EC countries.

TABLE 8.2. *Budget deficit of member states of unions (as a per cent of revenues)*

	Weighted mean	Unweighted mean
USA (1985)	+10.9	+4.6
Australia (1986–7)	−10.1	−9.1
West Germany (1987)	−6.4	−8.2
Canada (1982)	−0.4	−1.4
Switzerland (1986)	−1.3	−0.7
European Community (1988)	−10.1	−11.4

Note: A positive sign is a surplus, a negative sign a deficit. The weighted mean is obtained by weighting the deficits with the share of the member state in the union's GDP.
Source: Lamfalussy (1989: 102–24).

[5] For a recent formalization of the incentives of governments in multi-party systems, see Alesina and Tabellini (1987) and Persson and Svenson (1989). A classic analysis is Buchanan and Tullock (1962).

The most striking feature of Table 8.2 is the fact that the *average* budgetary deficits of the member states in monetary unions tend to be lower than the average deficit of independent countries in the EC.[6] This suggests that on average the existence of a union adds constraints to the size of the budget deficits of the member states. Thus, it appears that the no-monetization constraint is a powerful disincentive against running large budget deficits. It therefore seems that governments of member states of a monetary union face a 'harder' budget constraint than sovereign nations. The latter are confronted with 'softer' budget constraints and therefore have a stronger incentive to run deficits.

It should also be noted that, except in the case of Germany, in none of the monetary unions analysed in Table 8.2 does the federal authority impose restrictions on the budget deficits of the member states. In the Federal Republic the federal govern-ment can limit the borrowing requirements of the *Länder* with the consent of their representatives in the Bundesrat. This provision, however, has been invoked only twice (in 1971 and 1973).[7]

Whereas federally imposed limits are rare, one frequently finds *self-imposed* constitutional limits on state and *Länder* budget deficits. In fact, in the US the majority of the states have introduced such constitutional limitations. One possible inter-pretation for the frequency of self-imposed limits is that they may help to improve the reputation and the creditworthiness of the states in the capital markets, and therefore reduce the cost of borrowing.[8]

The evidence of Table 8.2 is of course not conclusive. More research should be carried out to find out whether the difference observed between the average deficits of member states of monetary unions and the average deficits of sovereign nations can be generalized to different time-periods and a larger sample of countries. At the very least, the results of Table

[6] This is also confirmed by Paul Van Rompuy *et al.* (1990).

[7] Van Rompuy *et al.* (1990: 19).

[8] As discussed earlier, von Hagen (1990) has argued that these constitutional limits on the budget deficits have been relatively ineffective. This would then suggest that, if perceived as ineffective in the capital markets, these constitu-tional restrictions should have a low effect on the risk premium.

8.2 suggest that the idea that in monetary unions member states have a strong incentive to create excessive levels of government debt is not corroborated by the facts of the 1980s.

In a recent paper Moesen and Van Rompuy (1990) provide additional indirect evidence for the hypothesis that the size of deficits depends on the 'softness' of the budget constraint. They classify industrial countries according to the degree of centralization of total government spending. The hypothesis tested is that more centralized governments face a softer budget constraint than decentralized governments. This is so because in centralized countries a larger part of total government spending can potentially be financed by the issue of money. In decentralized countries, however, a larger part of government spending occurs through lower-level authorities who lack the access to monetary financing. Moesen and Van Rompuy find evidence for this hypothesis: during the period 1973–86 the total government deficits in centralized countries increased faster than in decentralized ones. Put differently, during a period when government budgets were negatively affected by supply shocks and economic recession, the countries with more decentralized governments faced a stronger pressure to reduce spending and/or increase taxes than countries with more centralization of government functions.[9]

6. Conclusion

According to the theory of optimum currency areas, a monetary union in Europe should go together with some centralization of the national budgets. In particular, the unemployment benefit system and a significant part of income taxes should be centralized. Such a centralization of the budgetary process allows for *automatic* transfers to regions and countries hit by negative shocks.

It is quite unlikely that a significant centralization of the national budgets will be achieved in the near future in the

[9] Roubini and Sachs (1989) have identified other institutional features that have led to different trends in budget deficits, i.e. the degree of political cohesion of the governments in power.

Community. For some observers, in particular those who published the MacDougall Report, this means that it would be advisable to postpone further steps towards monetary unification.

Monetary unification in Europe appears to move forward despite the fact that no significant central European budget will exist. This poses the question of how national fiscal policies should be conducted in a monetary union.

In this chapter we discussed two views about this problem. The first one is based on the theory of optimum currency areas and suggests that national fiscal authorities should maintain a sufficient amount of flexibility and autonomy. The second has been formulated most forcefully in the Delors Report (and corresponds to what central bankers think about the subject). According to this view, the conduct of fiscal policies in the future monetary union will have to be disciplined by explicit rules on the size of the national budget deficits.

We have evaluated these two views. The optimum currency area view is probably overly optimistic about the possibility of national budgetary authorities using budget deficits as instruments to absorb negative shocks. Although there are situations in which countries will need the freedom to allow the budget to accommodate for these negative shocks, the sustainability of these policies severely limits their effectiveness.

We also argued, however, that the case for strict rules on the size of national government budget deficits is weak. There is no evidence that these rules are enforceable. In addition, the fact that national governments in a future monetary union will not have the same access to monetary financing as most of them have today, 'hardens' the budget constraint and reduces the incentives to run large budget deficits. The fear that national authorities will be less disciplined in a monetary union than in other monetary regimes does not seem to be well founded.

There remains the question of the conduct of fiscal policies during the transition to the monetary union. It may be advisable to allow entrance to the monetary union only to those countries that find themselves on a sustainable path of budget deficits. This is also the view taken by the drafters of the

---

[10] For such a proposal see Giovannini and Spaventa (1991).

Maastricht Treaty, who imposed strict budgetary criteria for entrance in the monetary union.

From the discussion of this chapter it will be clear that there are many unresolved issues concerning the design and the use of fiscal policies in a monetary union. There are two issues worth mentioning here. First, the future monetary union in Europe, if it comes about, will most likely have to operate without a centralized European budget of a significant size. As a result, there will be no automatic mechanism redistributing income between the regions. Assuming that labour mobility between countries will remain small, the adjustment mechanism needed to deal with asymmetric shocks will take the form of relative price changes. It is unclear today whether this mechanism will be flexible enough to deal with such disturbances. We cannot exclude the possibility that some countries will find it very difficult to adjust.

Secondly, many issues concerning the interaction between the European central bank and the national fiscal authorities will have to be resolved. It is one thing to legislate that the national authorities will have no access to monetary financing. It is quite another to enforce such a rule. When large countries are affected by negative disturbances the authorities of these countries are likely to pressure the European central bank to follow accommodative policies. Thus, the absence of a reliable mechanism able to deal with asymmetric shocks is likely to put a lot of pressure on the European monetary authorities. Some economists have argued that this may impose an inflationary bias on the future monetary union in Europe.

The decision to go ahead with monetary union has clearly been inspired by the political objective of European unification. In this dynamic towards political union, many objections expressed by economists, and formulated in this and in previous chapters, have been brushed aside. Whether this is a wise decision only the future will tell for sure.

References

Aizenman, J., and Frenkel, J. (1985) 'Optimal Wage Indexation, Foreign Exchange Intervention, and Monetary Policy', *American Economic Review*, 75: 402–23.

Alesina, A., and Tabellini, G. (1987) 'A Positive Theory of Fiscal Deficits and Government Debt in a Democracy', NBER Working Paper, 2308, Cambridge, Mass.

—— (1989) 'Politics and Business Cycles in Industrial Democracies', *Economic Policy*, 8: 55–98.

'All Saints' Day Manifesto', *The Economist*, 1 Nov. 1975.

Artis, M. J., and Taylor, M. P. (1988) 'Exchange Rates, Interest Rates, Capital Controls and the European Monetary System: Assessing the Track Record', in Giavazzi *et al.* (1988) *The European Monetary System*, Cambridge: CUP: 185–206.

Backus, D., and Driffill, J. (1985) 'Inflation and Reputation', *American Economic Review*, 75: 530–8.

Bade, R., and Parkin, M. (1978) 'Central Bank Laws and Monetary Policies: A Preliminary Investigation, The Australian Monetary System in the 1970s', Clayton: Monash University.

Balassa, B. (1961) *The Theory of Economic Integration*, London: Allen & Unwin.

Baldwin, R. (1989) 'On the Growth Effects of 1992', *Economic Policy*, 11.

Barro, R. (1972) 'Inflationary Finance and the Welfare Cost of Inflation', *Journal of Political Economy*, 80: 978–1001.

—— and Gordon, D. (1983) 'Rules, Discretion and Reputation in a Model of Monetary Policy', *Journal of Monetary Economics*, 12: 101–21.

Begg, D., and Wyplosz, C. (1987) 'Why the EMS? Dynamic Games and the Equilibrium Policy Regime', in R. Bryant and R. Portes (eds.), *Global Macroeconomics: Policy Conflict and Cooperation*, New York: St Martin's Press.

Bertola, G., and Svensson, L. (1991) 'Stochastic Devaluation Risk and the Empirical Fit of Target Zone Models', NBER Working Paper, 3576, Cambridge, Mass.

Boyd, C., Gielens, G., and Gros, D. (1990) 'Bid-Ask Spreads in the Foreign Exchange Markets', mimeo, Brussels.

Bruno, M., and Sachs, J. (1985) *Economics of Worldwide Stagflation*, Oxford: Basil Blackwell.

Buchanan, J., and Gordon, T. (1962) *The Calculus of Consent*, Ann Arbor: University of Michigan.

Buiter, W., and Kletzer, K. (1990) 'Reflections on the Fiscal Implications of a Common Currency', CEPR Discussion Paper 418.

Cagan, P. (1956) 'The Monetary Dynamics of Hyperinflation', in M. Friedman (ed.), *Studies in the Quantity Theory of Money*, Chicago, 25–117.

Calmfors, L., and Driffill, J. (1988) 'Bargaining Structure, Corporatism and Macroeconomic Performance', *Economic Policy*, 6: 13–61.

Carlin, W., and Soskice, D. (1990) *Macroeconomics and the Wage Bargain*, Oxford: OUP.

Cohen, D. (1983) 'La Coopération monétaire européenne: du SME à l'Union monétaire', *Revue d'économie financière*, 8/9.

—— and Wyplosz, C. (1989) 'The European Monetary Union: An Agnostic Evaluation', typescript.

Collins, S. (1988) 'Inflation and the European Monetary System', in Giavazzi *et al.* (1988), *The European Monetary System*, Cambridge: CUP, 112–36.

Committee on the Study of Economic and Monetary Union (the Delors Committee) (1989) *Report on Economic and Monetary Union in the European Community (Delors Report)* (with Collection of Papers), Luxemburg: Office for Official Publications of the European Communities.

Corden, M. (1972) 'Monetary Integration', *Essays in International Finance*, no. 93, Princeton.

David, P. (1985) 'CLIO and the Economics of QWERTY', *American Economic Review*, 75: 332–7.

De Cecco, M., and Giovannini, A. (eds.) (1989) *A European Central Bank? Perspectives on Monetary Unification after Ten Years of the EMS*, Cambridge: CUP.

De Grauwe, P. (1975) 'Conditions for Monetary Integration: A Geometric Interpretation', *Weltwirtschaftliches Archiv*, 111: 634–46.

—— (1983) *Macroeconomic Theory for the Open Economy*, Aldershot: Gower.

—— (1987) 'International Trade and Economic Growth in the EMS', *European Economic Review*, 31: 389–98.

—— (1988) 'Is the European Monetary System a DM-zone?' CEPR Discussion Paper, 297.

—— (1990) 'The Cost of Disinflation and the European Monetary System', *Open Economies Review*, 1: 147–73.

—— and Vanhaverbeke, W. (1990) 'Exchange Rate Experiences of Small EMS Countries. The Cases of Belgium, Denmark and the Netherlands', in V. Argy and P. De Grauwe (eds.), *Choosing an Exchange Rate Regime*, Washington DC: International Monetary Fund.

Demopoulos, G., Katsimbris, G., and Miller, S. (1987) 'Monetary Policy and Central Bank Financing of Government Budget Deficits: A Cross-Country Comparison', *European Economic Review*, 31: 1023–50.

Dornbusch, R. (1976) 'Money and Finance in European Integration', mimeo, Cambridge, Mass.: MIT.

—— and Fischer, S. (1978) *Macroeconomics*, New York: McGraw-Hill.

—— (1988) 'The European Monetary System, the Dollar and the Yen', in Giavazzi *et al.* (1988) *The European Monetary System*, Cambridge: CUP, 23–36.

Draft Treaty amending the Treaty establishing the European Economic Community, as published in Agence Europe, Europe Documents, 20 Dec. 1990.

Driffill, J. (1988) 'The Stability and Sustainability of the European Monetary System with Perfect Capital Markets', in Giavazzi *et al.* *(1988) The European Monetary System*, Cambridge: CUP, 211–18.

EC Commission (1977) Report of the Study Group on the Role of Public Finance in European Integration (MacDougall Report), Brussels.

—— (1988) 'The Economics of 1992', in *European Economy*, 35.

—— (1990) 'One market, One money', in *European Economy*, 44.

Eichengreen, B. (1990) 'Is Europe an Optimum Currency Area?', CEPR Discussion Paper, 478.

Fischer, S. (1982) 'Seigniorage and the Case for a National Money', *Journal of Political Economy*, 90/2: 295–307.

Fratianni, M. (1988) 'The European Monetary System: How Well has it Worked? Return to an Adjustable-Peg Arrangement', *Cato Journal*, 8: 477–501.

—— and Peeters, T. (eds.) (1978) *One Money for Europe*, London: Macmillan.

—— and von Hagen, J. (1990) 'German Dominance in the EMS: The Empirical Evidence', *Open Economies Review*, 1: 86–7.

Friedman, M. (1967) 'The Role of Monetary Policy', *American Economic Review*, 58/1, 1–17.

Froot, R., and Obstfeld, M. (1989) 'Exchange Rate Dynamics under Stochastic Regime Shifts', NBER Working Paper, 2835, Cambridge, Mass.

Giavazzi, F. and Giovannini, A. (1989) *Limiting Exchange Rate Flexibility: The European Monetary System*, Cambridge, Mass.: MIT Press.

—— Micossi, S., and Miller, M. (eds.) (1988) *The European Monetary System*, Cambridge: CUP.

—— and Pagano, M. (1985) 'Capital Controls and the European Monetary System', in *Capital Controls and Foreign Exchange Legislation*, Euromobiliare, Occasional Paper 1.

—— —— 'The Advantage of Tying One's Hands: EMS Discipline and Central Bank Credibility', *European Economic Review* 32: 1055–82.

—— and Spaventa, L. (1990) 'The "New" EMS', in P. De Grauwe and L. Papademos (eds.), *The European Monetary System in the 1990s*, London: Longman.

Giersch, H. (1973) 'On the Desirable Degree of Flexibility of Exchange Rates', *Weltwirtschaftliches Archiv*, 109: 191–213.

Giovannini, A., and Spaventa, L. (1961) 'Fiscal Rules in the European Monetary Union: A No-Entry Clause', CEPR Discussion Paper, 516.

Goodhart, C. (1989) '*The Delors Report*: Was Lawson's Reaction Justifiable?' London: Financial Markets Group, London School of Economics (unpublished).

Grilli, V. (1989) 'Seigniorage in Europe', in M. De Cecco and A. Giovannini.

Gros, D. (1990) 'Seigniorage and EMS Discipline', in P. De Grauwe and L. Papademos (eds.), *The European Monetary System in the 1990s*, London: Longman.

—— and Thygesen, N. (1988) 'The EMS: Achievements, Current Issues and Directions for the Future', CEPS Paper, 35, Brussels: Centre for European Policy Studies.

—— —— *European Monetary Integration: From the European Monetary System towards Monetary Union*, London: Longman (forthcoming).

Hayek, F. (1978) *Denationalization of Money*, London: Institute of Economic Affairs.

Holtfrerich, C.-L. (1989) 'The Monetary Unification Process in Nineteenth-Century Germany: Relevance and Lessons for Europe Today', in M. De Cecco and A. Giovannini (1989).

HM Treasury (1989) *An Evolutionary Approach to Economic and Monetary Union*, London: HMSO.

—— (1990) 'The Hard ECU Proposal', mimeo.

Ingram, J. (1959) 'State and Regional Payments Mechanisms', *Quarterly Journal of Economics*, 73: 619–32.

International Monetary Fund (1984) 'Exchange Rate Volatility and World Trade: A Study by the Research Department of the International Monetary Fund', *Occasional Papers*, 28.

Jozzo, A. (1989) 'The Use of the ECU as an Invoicing Currency', in P. De Grauwe and T. Peeters (eds.), *The ECU and European Monetary Integration*, London: Macmillan, 148–90.

Kaldor, N. (1966) *The Causes of the Slow Growth of the United Kingdom*, Cambridge: CUP.

Kenen, P. (1969) 'The Theory of Optimum Currency Areas: An Eclectic View', in R. Mundell and A. Swoboda (eds.), *Monetary Problems of the International Economy*, Chicago: University of Chicago Press.

Klein, B. (1978) 'Competing Monies, European Monetary Union and the Dollar', in Fratianni and Peeters (1978).

Krugman, P. (1987) 'Trigger Strategies and Price Dynamics in Equity and Foreign Exchange Markets', NBER Working Paper, 2459, Cambridge, Mass.

—— (1989) 'Differences in Income Elasticities and Trends in Real Exchange Rates', *European Economic Review*, 33/5: 1031–47.

—— (1990) 'Policy Problems of a Monetary Union', in P. De Grauwe, P. and L. Papademos (eds.), *The European Monetary System in the 1990s*, London: Longman.

—— (1991) *Geography and Trade*, Cambridge, Mass.: MIT Press.

Kydland, F., and Prescott, E. (1977) 'Rules Rather than Discretion: The Inconsistency of Optimal Plans', *Journal of Political Economy*, 85.

Lamfalussy, A. (1989) 'Macro-coordination of Fiscal Policies in an Economic and Monetary Union', in Committee for the Study of Economic and Monetary Union, *Report on Economic and Monetary Union (Delors Report)*, Luxemburg.

Lomax, D. (1989) 'The ECU as an Investment Currency,' in P. De Grauwe and T. Peeters (eds.), *The ECU and European Monetary Integration*, London: Macmillan, 119–38.

Ludlow, P. (1982) *The Making of the European Monetary System*, London: Butterworths.

Mastropasqua, C., Micossi, S., and Rinaldi, R. (1988) 'Interventions, Sterilization and Monetary Policy in the EMS Countries (1979–1987)', in Giavazzi *et al.* (1988), 252–87.

McDonald, I., and Solow, R. (1981) 'Wage Bargaining and Employment', *American Economic Review*, 71: 896–908.

Mélitz, J. (1985) 'The Welfare Cost of the European Monetary System', *Journal of International Money and Finance* 4: 485–506.

—— (1988) 'Monetary Discipline, Germany and the European Monetary System: A Synthesis', in F. Giavazzi, S. Micossi, and M. Miller (1988), 51–79.

Moesen, W., and Van Rompuy, P. (1990) 'The Growth of Government Size and Fiscal Decentralization', Paper prepared for the IIPF Congress, Brussels.

Mundell, R. (1961) 'A Theory of Optimal Currency Areas', *American Economic Review*, 51.

Myrdal, G. (1957) *Economic Theory and Underdeveloped Regions*, New York: Duckworth.

Neumann, M. (1990) 'Central Bank Independence as a Prerequisite of Price Stability', mimeo, University of Bonn.

OECD (1990) *Economic Outlook*, Paris.

Padoa-Schioppa, T. (1988) 'The European Monetary System: A Long-Term View', in F. Giavazzi, S. Micossi, and M. Miller (1988).

Parkin, M., and Bade, R. (1988) *Modern Macroeconomics*, 2nd edn., Oxford: Philip Allan.

Persson, T., and Svenson, L. (1989) 'Why a Stubborn Conservative would run a Deficit: Policy with Time Inconsistent Preferences', *Quarterly Journal of Economics*, 104.

Phelps, E. (1968) 'Money-Wage Dynamics and Labour Market Equilibrium', *Journal of Political Economy*, 76/4, 678–711.

Poole, W. (1970) 'Optimal Choice of Monetary Policy Instruments in a Simple Stochastic Macro Model', *Quarterly Journal of Economics*, 85.

Portes, R. (1989) 'Macroeconomic Policy Coordination and the European Monetary System', CEPR Discussion Paper, 342.

Rogoff, K. (1985a) 'Can Exchange Rate Predictability be Achieved without Monetary Convergence? Evidence from the EMS', *European Economic Review*, 28: 93–115.

—— (1985b) 'The Optimal Degree of Commitment to an Intermediate Monetary Target', *Quarterly Journal of Economics*, 100: 1169–90.

Romer, P. (1986) 'Increasing Returns and Long-Term Growth', *Journal of Political Economy*.

Roubini, N., and Sachs, J. (1989) 'Government Spending and Budget Deficits in the Industrial Countries', *Economic Policy*, 11: 100–32.

Russo, M., and Tullio, C. (1988) 'Monetary Policy Coordination within the European Monetary System: Is there a Rule?' in Giavazzi et al. (1988), 292–356.

Sachs, J., and Sala-i-Martin, X. (1989) 'Federal Fiscal Policy and Optimum Currency Areas', Working Paper, Cambridge, Mass.: Harvard University.

—— and Wyplosz, C. (1986) 'The Economic Consequences of President Mitterand', *Economic Policy*, 2.

Sachverständigenrat zur Begutachtung der Gesamtwirtschaftlichen Entwicklung, Sondergutachten, 20 Jan. 1990.

Salin, P. (ed.) (1984) *Currency Competition and Monetary Union*, The Hague: Martinus Nijhoff.

Sannucci, V. (1989) 'The Establishment of a Central Bank: Italy in the Nineteenth Century', in De Cecco and Giovannini (1989).

Sargent, T., and Wallace, N. (1981) 'Some Unpleasant Monetarist Arithmetic', Federal Reserve Bank of Minneapolis, *Quarterly Review*, 5: 1–17.

Steinherr, A. (1989) *Concrete Steps for Developing the ECU*, A report prepared by the ECU Banking Association Macrofinancial Study Group, Brussels.

Stiglitz, J., and Weiss, A. (1981) 'Credit Rationing in Markets with Imperfect Information', *American Economic Review*, 71: 393–410.

Straubhaar, T. (1988) 'International Labour Migration within a Common Market: Some Aspects of the EC Experience', *Journal of Common Market Studies*, 27.

Svensson, L. (1990) 'The Foreign Exchange Risk Premium in a Target Zone with Devaluation Risk', Seminar Paper, 475, Institute of International Economic Studies, University of Stockholm.

Thygesen, N. (1988) 'Decentralization and Accountability within the Central Bank: Any Lessons from the US Experience for the Potential Organization of a European Central Banking Institution?' (with comment by Jean-Jacques Rey), in P. De Grauwe and T. Peeters (eds.), *The ECU and European Monetary Integration*, Basingstoke: Macmillan, 91–118.

—— (1989) 'A European Central Banking System—Some Analytical and Operational Considerations', in Collection of Papers of *Delors Report*, 157–75.

Tower, E., and Willett, T. (1976) 'The Theory of Optimum Currency Areas and Exchange Rate Flexibility', *Special Papers in International Finance*, 11, Princeton, NJ: Princeton University.

Turnovsky, S. (1984) 'Exchange Market Intervention under Alternative Forms of Exogenous Disturbances', *Journal of International Economics*, 17: 279–97.

Ungerer, H., Evans, O., and Nyberg, P. (1986) 'The European Monetary System: Recent Developments', *Occasional Paper*, 48, International Monetary Fund, Washington DC.

van der Ploeg, F. (1991) 'Macroeconomic Policy Coordination during the Various Phases of Economic and Monetary Integration in Europe', in EC Commission, *European Economy*, Special Edn., 1.

Van Neder, N., and Vanhaverbeke, W. (1990) 'The Causes of Price Differences in the European Car Markets', International Economics Discussion Paper, University of Leuven.

Van Rompuy, P., Abraham, F., and Heremans, D. (1991) 'Economic Federalism and the EMU', EC Commission, *European Economy*, Special Edn., 1.

van Ypersele, J. (1985) *The European Monetary System*, Cambridge: Woodhead.

Vaubel, R. (1978) *Strategies for Currency Unification*, Kieler Studien, no. 156, Tübingen, Mohr & Siebeck.

—— 'Uberholte Glaubenssätze', *Wirtschaftsdienst*, 69, 276–9.

—— (1990) 'Currency Competition and European Monetary Integration', *Economic Journal*, 100, 936–46.

von Hagen, J., and Fratianni, M. (1990) 'Asymmetries and Realignments in the EMS', in P. De Grauwe and L. Papademos (eds.), *The European Monetary System in the 1990s*, Longman: London.

von Hagen, J. (1991*a*) 'A Note on the Empirical Effectiveness of Formal Fiscal Restraints', *Journal of Public Economics*, 44, 199–210.

—— (1991*b*) 'Fiscal Arrangements in a Monetary Union. Evidence from the US', Working Paper, Bloomington: Indiana University.

Walters, A. (1986) *Britain's Economic Renaissance*, Oxford University Press, Oxford.

Weber, A. (1990) 'European Economic and Monetary Union and Asymmetric and Adjustment Problems in the European Monetary System: Some Empirical Evidence', Siegen: University of Siegen, Discussion Paper, 9–90.

Williamson, J. (1983) *The Exchange Rate System*, Institute of International Economics, Washington, DC.

Wyplosz, C. (1989) 'Asymmetry in the EMS: Intentional or Systemic?', *European Economic Review*, 33: 310–20.

—— (1991) 'Monetary Union and Fiscal Policy Discipline', EC Commission, *European Economy*, Special Edn., 1.

Zimmerman, H. (1989) 'Fiscal Equalization between States in West Germany', *Government and Policy*, 7: 385–93.

Index